THE AGONY
OF
CHRISTIANITY

Miguel de Unamuno

THE AGONY
OF
CHRISTIANITY

104646

Translated, with an introduction, by
KURT F. REINHARDT

FREDERICK UNGAR PUBLISHING CO.
NEW YORK

Printed in the United States of America

Library of Congress Catalog Card Number 60-13989

CONTENTS

INTRODUCTION

I

The reader who wants to gain insight into the complex mind and the anguished soul of Miguel de Unamuno will do well to contemplate for a moment the situation of Roman Catholicism and of the Roman Catholic intellectual in the contemporary world. Until quite recently, modern Catholicism in Europe and in North America lived by and large in the religious climate created by the Council of Trent (1545-1563) and the "Counter-Reformation." In the course of the post-Tridentine centuries the lines marked by confessional or denominational separation had hardened to such an extent that communication between the divided camps had become almost impossible. The ecumenical zeal which had animated the minds of "Christian Humanists" from Nicholas of Cusa, Erasmus, and St. Thomas More to Leibniz, was all but forgotten. In their firmly entrenched positions both Protestants and Catholics had developed "closed" systems of dogmatic theology, which were essentially defensive and thus without that "overtness" which is an indispensable condition for any amount of mutual understanding or any significant "dialogue." The "Third Power," that is, the force of the centuries old Christian Humanism of the West, seemed practically extinct.[1]

As far as contemporary Catholicism is concerned, the phrase of the "Catholic ghetto" and of the corresponding "ghetto-mentality" (a phrase coined originally, if I remember correctly, by Carl Muth [1867-1944], the founder and editor of the German Catholic review "Hochland"), described the situation quite aptly.

The bigoted Roman Catholic and Protestant who are the targets of Unamuno's scornful attacks are "ghetto-Christians," whose fear of mingling with and facing the challenges of the modern world has caused them to seek shelter behind the protective cortex of a merely conventional and therefore existentially meaningless religiosity. The result has been a desiccated and atrophied religious faith with some distinctly puritanical and at times even neo-manichaean features. The post-Reformation Catholic in particular gradually came to regard his relationship to God, to his neighbor, and to the world as inflexibly fixed and to look upon the supernatural as a sort of life insurance policy which permitted him to live securely in a world, a society, and a Church in which all prob-

[1] Cf. Friedrich Heer, *Die Dritte Kraft* (Frankfurt a.M.: S. Fischer Verlag, 1959).

lems were shoved aside because all questions were already neatly answered.

If Unamuno were still alive, it would no doubt please him immensely to notice that the contemporary Christian—Protestant and Catholic alike—does no longer enjoy this kind of security, that man, as Unamuno had demanded, had been plunged into the ocean of life, deprived of every anchorage, so that he might learn again what it means to exist as a human being.

Risk and uncertainty have become the rule rather than an exception in the life of the contemporary Christian, who realizes that religious faith is dynamic rather than static, that it has to be tried and tested and reconquered from day to day, and who therefore feels inclined to exclaim with that father in the Gospel: "I do believe; Lord, help my unbelief!" (Mark 9:23). "Conscious or not," writes the late Jesuit palaeontologist Pierre Teilhard de Chardin (1881-1955), ". . . a fundamental anguish of being . . . strikes in the depths of all our hearts and is the undertone of all our conversations. . . . 'There is nothing new under the sun,' say the despairing. But what about you, O thinking man? . . . O man of the twentieth century, how does it happen that you are waking up to horizons and are susceptible to fears that your forefathers never knew?" [2]

[2] Pierre Teilhard de Chardin, *The Phenomenon of Man*. With an Introduction by Sir Julian Huxley (New York: Harper & Brothers, 1959), p. 226 sq.

Some French writers of the *renouveau catholique* have made a significant distinction between the "protected" and the "exposed" Christian, and an astute neo-Calvinist like Karl Barth espouses and endorses the position of the "exposed" Christian when he says in effect that a living faith, which finds itself challenged again and again, has for this very reason a deeper understanding of the non-believer than the smug and self-assured "Christian," whose "faith" can hardly be distinguished from indifference. The identical thought was given its most forceful expression by Dostoevsky in that memorable conversation of Stavrogin (the protagonist of the novel *The Possessed*) with the Russian Orthodox Bishop Tikhon, where the Bishop tells his visitor that atheism stands on the penultimate step of the ladder that leads to faith, whereas indifference is farthest removed from faith.

Now indifference is one thing of which Unamuno could never be accused. It is difficult to gauge what would have been his reaction to the fact that the life of the present-day Roman Catholic—even in his own beloved Spain—has often the same tragic overtones as the life of the orthodox or neo-orthodox Lutheran and Calvinist.[3]

It is, however, when we turn toward that soul-

[3] Cf. for striking evidence the recent theological novel by the young Spanish Jesuit priest, José Luis Martín Descalzo, *The Frontier of God* (New York: Alfred Knopf, 1959).

shaking experience which since the publication
of Kierkegaard's 'Sickness Unto Death" is commonly referred to as "existential despair," that an
essential difference in attitude on the part of "exposed" Protestants and "exposed" Catholics becomes very obvious. For Martin Luther, for Kierkegaard, and for the early "dialectical" theology
of Karl Barth, despair functions as an original
motivating force engendering faith; and even after
the "leap" into faith or into "the paradox" (the
incarnation of eternity in time, in the person of
Christ) has been made, despair remains an ever
open possibility and a constant threat. St. Thomas
Aquinas, on the other hand, remains to this day
the spokesman of Roman Catholic theology when
he calls despair "a vice" and "a sin": *"motus
desperationis est vitiosus et peccatum"* (*Summa
theologica,* IIa, IIae, XX, 1). Thomas goes so far
as to refer to despair—considered subjectively—
as "the greatest and most dangerous sin," although
he adds that "objectively" (or in the absolute
sense) infidelity and hate are greater sins.

Now if we look upon the phenomenon of existential despair from a psychological point of
view, there is hardly any doubt that such despair
(in the sense in which Kierkegaard understood
it) must not of necessity be a fatal sickness of
mind and soul, because it may and can be healed
by faith; and when this happens, despair has actually proven to be a starter on the road to faith.
There is even less doubt, however, that despair

may and often does lead to the extirpation of faith. At any rate, no Roman Catholic would or could with Luther and Kierkegaard look upon despair as a sort of pre-condition of faith. And what is said here of despair applies *mutatis mutandis* to Unamuno's "agony," which is well-nigh synonymous with existential despair. In this as in several other respects Unamuno shows his close spiritual kinship with some of the major protagonists of original and modern Protestantism.

It would seem that Gabriel Marcel—the leading Catholic existential thinker—points to a solution of this knotty problem when he contends that Christian *hope* arises in most instances from a critical "limit-situation" of "threat" or "danger"; that "the foundation of hope lies in the consciousness of a situation which invites despair." [4] Such "limit-situations" are, according to Karl Jaspers, given in suffering, guilt, strife, sickness, and in the inescapable certainty of death. "The conditions of hope," says Kant, "seem to coincide with the conditions of despair." Or, expressed paradoxically in the language of Karl Barth, "True hope is born when there is no longer any hope at all." [5] In other words, then, the Catholic existential thinker—in contradistinction to the Protestant ex-

[4] Cf. Gabriel Marcel, *Être et Avoir* (Paris: Aubier, 1935), pp. 55, 150.

[5] Cf. Karl Barth, *Kirchliche Dogmatik* (München: Chr. Kaiser Verlag, 1957), IV, p. 508.

istential thinker—affirms that man is capable of despair but capable also of overcoming the temptation to succumb to despair, by virtue of faith and hope. He asserts moreover that faith and hope do not require despair as a necessary pre-condition.

All existentially committed Christians are today willing and eager to endorse Kierkegaard's demand that the individual Christian become "contemporary with Christ" by "repeating" as it were in the act of faith the inward history of the human race, from the pre-Christian state of "silent despair" to the Christian state of promise, hope and fulfillment. In other words, faith can no more be "inherited" than can hope and love, so that in this realm of spiritual realities every individual has to start from the beginning.

Among the most original, influential, and provocative thinkers of the second half of the nineteenth century are (aside from *Sören Kierkegaard*) *Friedrich Nietzsche* and *Cardinal John Henry Newman*. Notwithstanding the fact that Kierkegaard and Newman were believing Christians, while Nietzsche was a self-styled atheist and "Anti-Christ," they had a great deal in common in their understanding and interpretation of some of the most basic problems of human existence. Their challenges bore rich fruit in contemporary "existential" theology—both Protestant and Catholic (Karl Barth, Emil Brunner, Rudolf Bultmann,

Reinhold Niebuhr; Erich Przywara, S.J., Hans Urs von Balthasar, Henri de Lubac, S.J., among others—and "existential" philosophy (Martin Heidegger, Karl Jaspers, Martin Buber, Jean-Paul Sartre, Maurice Merleau-Ponty, Francis Jeanson). It was Kierkegaard in particular who made possible not only a genuine rebirth of an intensely personalist Protestantism but who also contributed vitally to the opening up of new perspectives in modern and contemporary Catholicism. And the Danish thinker exerted an equally strong influence on some of the most prominent literary figures in Europe, such as Henrik Ibsen (*Brand, Peer Gynt, Emperor and Galilaean*), Rainer Maria Rilke (*Duino Elegies, Sonnets to Orpheus*), and Miguel de Unamuno.

In the life and work of Newman, too, the "existential" note and emphasis are unmistakable, and in the circles of an "open," humanistically inspired Catholicism Newman's influence is comparable to that of Kierkegaard. The similarity of the challenge extends even to Kierkegaard's famous "either/or": "I came to the conclusion," writes Newman, "that there was no medium, in true philosophy, between Atheism and Catholicity, and that a perfectly consistent mind . . . must embrace either the one or the other." [6] And when the

[6] John Henry Newman, *Apologia pro vita sua* (London, 1946; with an Introduction by Maisie Ward), p. 133.

leader of the "Oxford Movement" back to Rome asks himself about the reasons for his religious faith, he answers: . . . "it is because I believe in myself; for I feel it impossible to believe in my own existence . . . without believing also in Him, Who lives as a Personal, All-seeing, All-judging Being in my conscience." [7] And again he says: "Without self-knowledge you have no root in yourselves personally; you may endure for a time, but under affliction or persecution your faith will not last. This is why many in this age (and in every age) become infidels . . . ; they cast off the form of truth, because it never has been to them more than a form." [8]

It is thus an incontestable fact that, in following the incentives of such "existential" and personalist thinkers as Kierkegaard and Newman, both Protestant and Catholic theology are placing increasing emphasis on "being-in" or "living-in" the Truth and correspondingly less emphasis on the categories of abstract notional knowledge. The "testimony" of "the witness" (G. Marcel) appears as more important than any purely rational demonstration or any of the rational preambles of faith. Religion is no longer felt as a guarantor of a sheltered life, of bourgeois security and moderate happiness. This is why *Simone Weil* voices

[7] Newman, *ibid.*

[8] Newman, *Parochial and Plain Sermons* (London, 1882), vol. I, p. 55.

the religious experience of many contemporary God-seekers and even of many orthodox believers when she speaks of two distinct planes of human existence: the ordinary, normal human life, and the quite different rhythm and dynamism of an extra-ordinary, highly personalized religious destiny and vocation. While no human being should be deprived of the "mixed goods" (*metaxú*) of fatherland, tradition, and family life, there are exceptional human situations in which (to use Kierkegaard's phrase) "the ethical must be suspended": the one who, like Abraham, "the knight of faith," is singled out by God for suffering and sacrifice, must do without a sheltered home, must live "in fear and trembling" as a stranger in exile and in solitude. And such abandonment must be accepted and lived without palliatives, for the ways of God and the ways to God pass through radical doubt, temptation (Luther's *Anfechtung*), guilt, shipwreck, and total dereliction. According to Simone Weil, it is only when the cry, "My God, my God, why hast Thou forsaken me?" breaks forth from the lips of the sacrificed one, that he shall find beatitude in the grace and love of God, in the very midst of abandonment and disgrace.

This phenomenological description of the religious experience of the "extra-ordinary" Christian fits closely the religious mentality of Unamuno. Since he called Kierkegaard *"hermano"* (his brother), he might have recognized in Simone Weil his spiritual sister. Contrary to the assertion of his more intolerant biographers, interpreters, and critics,[9] Unamuno was not a "modernist," although he did sympathize with some of the ideas of Loisy, Fogazzaro, Döllinger, and Tyrell. While the Modernists were striving for a reconciliation and harmonization of Catholic dogma and modern science, by means of adapting the contents of dogma to the findings of science and, more generally, to the social and moral climate of the modern age, Unamuno was not interested in any kind of conciliation or harmonization. The intellectual climate in which he lived and breathed was that of existential contradiction, incertitude, discord, doubt, and agony: in short, "the tragic sense of life." In his best known work, which bears this title, he wrote: "That pure faith, free of all dogma, of which I formerly talked so much, is a phantasm. . . . Faith stands in need of some material substrate in which it can exercise itself." This is clearly an anti-modernist thesis. It is evident that the solution proposed by Modernism was too facile to suit Unamuno's taste: it tended to dissolve dogma by eliminating the "antithesis" and therewith the elements of tragedy, despair, and agony. For Unamuno, faith can rise only "from the ground of the abyss."

The same Unamuno who said that the philoso-

[9] Cf. especially Nemesio González Caminero, S.J., *Unamuno. Trayectoria de su ideología y de su crisis religiosa* (Comillas [Santander]: Universidad Pontificia, 1948).

phy of Kant had found no acceptance in Spain
because "Kantianism is Protestant, while we Spaniards are fundamentally Catholic," felt all during
his life a strong inclination toward orthodox and
neo-orthodox Protestantism. He sympathized not
only with the religious experience of Kierkegaard
but equally with that of Martin Luther, with the
religious ideas of Huguenots and Jansenists as
well as with those embodied in the neo-Calvinism
of Karl Barth and Emil Brunner.

J. L. Aranguren argues convincingly that Luther, Pascal, Kierkegaard, and Unamuno represent four successive stages of a religious faith
that grows progressively more anguished and
problematical.[10] In Pascal's religious experience,
human existence finds itself confronted with "the
naught" for the first time: he saw that man, oc-
cupying as he does an intermediate position in
the universe—between the infinitesimal and the
infinite—is surrounded and threatened by "the
naught" on both sides; "he is an All in relation
to Nothingness, and he is a Nothingness in relation to the All." [11] For Kierkegaard, who was an
authentic lay theologian, God and Christ were
still absolute and ultimate realities—the absolute

[10] José Luis L. Aranguren, *Catolicismo y Protes-
tantismo como formas de existencia* (Madrid: Revista
de Occidente, 1952), p. 196.

[11] Cf. William Barrett, *Irrational Man. A Study in
Existential Philosophy.* (New York: Doubleday, 1958),
p. 103.

measure. For Unamuno, on the other hand, it is man who becomes the measure, while God exists solely as the guarantor of the immortality of the human soul. In Nietzsche and Sartre, finally, the "man-god" appropriates the attributes (especially the *"a-seitas"*) of the "God-Man, and the act of faith is replaced by a *"creatio ex nihilo"* of the human person and its moral imperatives.

To the metaphysico-anthropological question, "What is Man?", Unamuno answers: "Hunger of immortality." The essence of Catholicism is for him the "immortalization" of man, and "the sacrament of the Eucharist is the immortalizing agent *par excellence* and therefore the axis of popular Catholic piety." [12] To save himself from death, from "nihilation," from Nothingness, the Catholic Christian of Unamuno ventures the desperate Kierkegaardian "leap" into the paradox of faith. In Unamuno's own words, "That terrible secret, that mysterious will of God which translates itself into the dogma of predestination—the same idea which inspired Luther's concept of the *Servum arbitrium* (the enslaved will) and imparts to Calvinism its tragic sense—is at bottom nothing but that incertitude, linked with despair, which forms the basis of faith." [13] Faith, then—as is the case in Luther's *theologia crucis*—is born of anguish and despair: "It is not rational necessity but vital anguish which leads us to believe in

[12] Unamuno, *Ensayos,* II, p. 715.
[13] Unamuno, *Ensayos,* II, p. 766 sq.

God." [14] And, like Luther and Kierkegaard, Unamuno sees in despair the only means to arrive at "fiducial faith" and therewith at hope: "I have become accustomed to draw hope out of despair. And I don't mind if the fools and philistines cry, 'Paradox'!" [15]

It is obvious of course that Unamuno's "existential" and "fiducial" faith is incompatible with the Roman Catholic definition of faith, and the Spanish thinker had no illusions about this. His paradoxical faith is coextensive and coexistent with radical doubt. In the main character of his novel *San Manuel Bueno, mártir* (1931), Unamuno presented a tragic embodiment of the man, the priest, "the saint," who desperately *wants* to believe but cannot believe. This is why Unamuno could say: "I am convinced that I have put into [this novel] the entire tragic sense of everyday life." And in the *Essays* we read: "It is necessary to plunge men into the depth of the ocean and leave them to themselves, so that they may learn to swim, to become human beings. . . . And if you should drown in God, what does it matter? Those anxieties, tribulations and doubts of which you are so much afraid, are the living and eternal waters which will rouse you from the illusive quiet wherein you are dying hour by hour. Allow yourself . . . to sink to the ground, to lose conscious-

[14] Unamuno, *Ensayos*, II, p. 824.
[15] Unamuno, *Ensayos*, II, p. 398.

ness, and remain like a sponge, so that you may be swept back to the surface of the waters and find yourself at home with sight and touch and feeling in the element of the ocean." [16]

Unamuno—perhaps in order to gain a foothold in a supra-personal reality—projected his own religious experience into that of the Spanish people. Thus he calls despair "something genuinely Spanish . . . , a specifically Spanish form of despair, the foundation of hope, . . . perhaps even a hope without a faith, an absurd and mad hope." [17] Such an absurd and mad hope is also the quintessence of Unamuno's philosophy of *Quijotismo*, that is, his intensely personal interpretation of that idealism which possesses the *caballero de la triste figura*, which by a *tour de force* is made to stand for the *Weltanschauung* of the Spanish people and the Spanish nation: "There exists," we read in *The Tragic Sense of Life*, "a certain figure, a comically tragic figure, a figure in which we can see the profoundly tragic sense of the human comedy—the figure of Our Lord Don Quijote, the Spanish Christ, in whom is enshrined the immortal soul of my people. Perhaps the passion and death of [Don Quijote] is the passion and death of the Spanish people. Their death and their resurrection. And there exists a Quijotic philosophy, even a Quijotic metaphysics,

[16] Unamuno, *Ensayos*, II, p. 260 sq.
[17] Unamuno, *Ensayos*, II, p. 482.

logic, ethics, and religion—a Spanish-Catholic-Quijotic religiosity." [18]

To justify such extravagant generalizations, Unamuno makes a distinction between "popular Spanish Catholicism" and "ecclesiastical or Roman Catholicism." And he discerns "the tragic sense of life" in popular Catholicism, citing as evidence the tragic, "agonic" character of the representations of Christ and of the *Mater Dolorosa* in Spanish painting and sculpture. The Spanish Christ and the Spanish Virgin Mother, he says, are all as tragic and "agonic" as "that Christ of Velázquez, who is forever dying but never dead." [19]

Generally speaking, Unamuno accuses Roman Catholicism of having from the outset attempted "to link in marriage these two most incompatible things: the Gospel and Roman Law." The result was "that monstrous thing known as Canon Law." [20]

These views, especially as far as the totally negative evaluation of Canon Law is concerned, coincide almost to the letter with those of Luther. Though it is true that Unamuno's critique of Protestantism is in many respects as severe or even severer than that of official Catholicism, the

[18] Unamuno, *Del sentimiento trágico de la vida en los hombres y en los pueblos* (Madrid, 1913), p. 275.
[19] Unamuno, *Ensayos,* II, p. 718.—Cf. also the poem *El Cristo de Velázquez* (Madrid, 1920).
[20] Unamuno, *Ensayos,* I, pp. 251, 973.

target of his anti-Protestant attacks is never the "authentic" Protestantism of Luther, Calvin or Jansenius but always the diluted, flabby, sugar-coated and rationalized Liberal Protestantism of the nineteenth century.

In concluding and summarizing these casual observations concerning Unamuno's religious experience, it may be stated that in speaking of the shortcomings of Roman Catholicism, Unamuno had primarily in mind the religious mentality created by the Counter-Reformation. He castigated in particular the "closed" and rigidly systematized dogmatic theology to which he was exposed in his youth in his native Spain—a mentality which his rugged personalism came to detest. There is, however, as J. L. Aranguren points out, another Unamuno, who is the legitimate heir of Christian-Catholic Humanism and who is not so much the brother of the Protestant Reformers as he is the brother of Fray Luis de León (and perhaps the brother also of San Juan de la Cruz and Santa Teresa of Avila).[21]

II

Don Miguel de Unamuno y Jugo was born on September 29, 1864 in Bilbao, the capital of the Basque Province of Biscay. He received his elementary and secondary schooling in his native

[21] Cf. José Luis L. Aranguren, *op. cit.*, p. 208.

city and, in 1880, entered the University of
Madrid to study philosophy and the humanities.
In 1891 he obtained a professorship in Greek
Language and Literature at the University of
Salamanca and became Rector of this institution
in 1901. In addition to holding this high admin-
istrative office, he taught the History of the Cas-
tilian language. In 1914, Unamuno was relieved
of his position as Rector because he had pub-
licly favored the cause of the Allies in the war
against Germany. He was, however, subsequently
elected Vice-Rector of the university. In 1924,
Unamuno was exiled to Fuerteventura, one of the
Canary Islands, because of his violent opposition
to the military dictatorship of Primo de Rivera.
From there he managed to escape by boat to
France. Even when he was pardoned a short
time later, he refused to return to Spain, at least
for the time being, despite the fact that in his
exile he was separated from his wife and children. Instead, he went first to Paris and, in August
1925, to the Pyrenean bordertown of Hendaye.

In February, 1930, after the fall of Primo
de Rivera, Unamuno returned to Spain and was
reinstated in his chair at the University of Salamanca. When, in April, 1931, the Spanish Republic was proclaimed, he was officially exon-
erated and was elected a member of the *Cortes
Constituentes*. Soon, however, he began to look
upon the Spanish Republic with the same mis-
givings, suspicion, and scepticism that he had felt

with respect to the Monarchy and the interim military dictatorship. Being by nature and inclination an a-political individual, Unamuno felt that all three régimes had betrayed the soul and the spirit of Spain and of Christianity.

The outbreak of civil war could hardly have come as a surprise to Unamuno. He lived through this cruel and bloody internecine slaughter in semi-seclusion in his official mansion in Salamanca. What was happening to Spain "mortally wounded his heart," and yet he had to look on, condemned to inaction and condemned to soliloquize, for once again he found himself alone, beyond all frontiers and horizons, a victim of a "sickness unto death." Unamuno died of a heart ailment on December 31, 1936. He used to say that it was his hope and desire to live to the age of ninety, but he was only seventy-two when death came.

III

In the rich and variegated *oeuvre* of Unamuno the philosophico-theological works are in a category by themselves. Four of these stand out from the rest: *The Life of Don Quijote and Sancho* (1905); *The Tragic Sense of Life in Men and Peoples* (1913 [Engl. tr. 1921]); and *The Agony of Christianity* (French ed. 1925; Spanish ed. 1930). Chronologically, the *Don Quijote* belongs to the early period, *The Tragic Sense of Life* to the middle period, and *The Agony of Christi-*

anity to the final period of Unamuno's life. In *The Tragic Sense of Life* he comes closest to formulating a "creed" when he says: "My work . . . , my mission is to destroy everyone's faith: faith in affirmation, faith in negation, and faith in indifferent abstention, and this is so because I have faith in faith; and so it is my mission to wage war against all those who live resigned, be it to Catholicism, to rationalism, or to agnosticism."

Augustín Esclasans tells us in his biography of Unamuno that the Spanish thinker experienced a severe religious crisis in 1897, a crisis which brought him to the crossroads where he had to choose between anarchism and Christianity. The following day, we are told, Unamuno went to a Dominican monastery in Salamanca and remained in seclusion for three days. The first hours of his retreat he spent on his knees, in fervent and anguished supplication. While in the Dominican cloister, the only books he perused were the Bible and the *Confessions* of St. Augustine. If we take the author's word for it, similar religious crises recurred periodically in Unamuno's life.[22] And it might be well for us to remember that Unamuno was a Basque, that is, a man of the racial timber of St. Ignatius (Iñigo) of Loyola, who himself was no stranger to existential crises!

The spiritual crises of Unamuno are reflected most directly and most movingly in his philo-

[22] Agustín Esclasans, *Miguel de Unamuno* (Buenos Aires: Editorial Juventud, 1947), p. 112 sq.

sophico-religious works and in none of them (with the exception perhaps of the philosophico-theological novel, *San Manuel Bueno, mártir*) with more tragic overtones than in *The Agony of Christianity*. This anguished treatise is the work of an aging, a suffering, and an angry man. The things which he burns here are the same things which at one time or other he had loved and adored. "Behind his paradoxes," says Agustín Esclasans, ". . . there is always hiding a love, a passion for the objects of his attack." [23]

The Agony of Christianity was written in exile, in Paris, in 1925, and the book was immediately translated into French by Unamuno's admiring friend, Jean Cassou. The text actually presents several variations on one main theme—one of Unamuno's favorite and most frequently quoted Gospel sayings: "I do believe; Lord, help my unbelief!" (Mark 9:23). This anguished exclamation of a father whose son was possessed by an evil spirit but who was cleansed and healed by Christ, expresses most tersely the nature of Unamuno's terrible "agonic" doubt and his simultaneous fervent "will to believe."

There is no doubt that Unamuno, like Dostoevsky, was a man possessed, haunted, and tortured by the idea of God and by the problem of Christianity. The agony which Christianity suffered in the soul of Unamuno consisted largely in

[23] Agustín Esclasans, *op. cit.*, p. 114.

the disheartening conviction (based on personal experience) that reason was entirely powerless to penetrate to the heart of the mysteries of faith and of the supernatural, while at the same time there persisted in his soul the hunger and unquenchable thirst for the immortality of the soul and the resurrection of the body. In the last analysis, then, the agony of Christianity is reduced for Unamuno to a hopeless and frustrating (because non-resolvable) dialectic of faith versus reason. In despair, in "fear and trembling," Unamuno was seeking the only way out of the dilemma that appeared open to the "exposed Christian": Tertullian's *"credo quia absurdum."* In his paradoxical faith Unamuno tried to picture God as a projection of his own self, magnified to infinity. The immortal God is envisaged as the sublime and exalted symbol of personal immortality, as the Creator Who with His eternal *"fiat"* saves man from the void of Nothingness. And thus, the agony of man on his earthly pilgrimage consists in the ever repetitive gain and loss, rise and fall of his slowly progressing eternalization. To give to man in his agony this impetus and *élan*, God must "not only exist, but super-exist, in order to sustain in this way our own fragile existence."

K. F. R.

THE AGONY
OF
CHRISTIANITY

"Muero porque no muero."

"I am dying because I cannot die."

Santa Teresa de Jesús

INTRODUCTION TO THE FRENCH EDITION OF 1925

Christianity represents that universal spirit which has its roots in the deepest inwardness of human individuality. The Jesuits assert that Christianity is concerned with resolving the "business" of our individual and personal salvation, and though it is principally the Jesuits who are wont to speak in this manner—thus making of religion a problem of "economics" applied to things divine —we may well accept their point of view as a provisional postulate.

Since Christianity is a strictly individual and thus simultaneously a universal problem, I feel myself compelled, dear reader, to expound briefly the personal and private circumstances in which the writing of this treatise has been undertaken.

The military tyranny which oppresses my poor Spanish fatherland had confined me to the island of Fuerteventura,* where I had an opportunity to enrich my religious and even mystical inner ex-

* The second largest of the Canary Islands (in Portuguese: Fortaventura).—*Translator*

perience. I was taken from there to French soil by a French sailboat, so that I could settle here in Paris, where I am now writing this in a sort of cloistered cell, not far from the Arc de l'Etoile. Here in Paris, a city filled to the brim with history, teeming with social and public life, it is almost impossible to find refuge in some infra-historical (and therefore also supra-historical) corner. Here I cannot contemplate the high Sierra, crowned with snow during the greater part of the year, which at Salamanca gave nourishment to the roots of my soul; nor the vast plain, that steppe which at Palencia—the place where my eldest son has his home—gives repose to my spirit; nor the sea from which at Fuerteventura I saw the sun rise every day. And even this river, the Seine, is, alas, not the Nervión of my native Bilbao, where one feels the pulse of the sea, the ebb and flow of its tides. Since my arrival in Paris I have been nourishing myself in this cell of mine from books somewhat chosen at random, trusting to chance; for chance is the root principle of freedom.

It was in these personal circumstances of, if I may say so, a distinctly religious and Christian character that M. P.-L. Couchoud approached me to ask me that I prepare for him a notebook for his collection titled "Christianity"; and it was he who, among other titles, suggested that of "The Agony of Christianity." He was familiar with my book, "The Tragic Sense of Life."

At the time M. P.-L. Couchoud surprised me with his request I had just been reading Charles Maurras' *Enquête sur la monarchie* (Inquiry into the Nature of Monarchy)—far removed indeed from the spirit of the Gospels—wherein he serves us in tin cans a dish of rotten meat from the slaughterhouse of the late Count Joseph de Maistre.*

In that profoundly anti-Christian book I read the following excerpt from the program of the *Action Française* of 1903: "A true nationalist places his country above all else; he therefore understands, discusses, resolves all political questions *in relation to the national interest.*" When I read this I remembered the saying, "My kingdom is not of this world," and I thought that for a true Christian—if such a thing as a good Christian is conceivable in public life—every question, whether of a political or any other nature, must be understood, discussed, and resolved as it relates to the individual's interest in eternity and in eternal salvation. And what if one's fatherland were to perish? A Christian's fatherland is not of this world. A Christian must be willing to sacrifice his country to the Truth.

The Truth! ". . . One no longer deceives anyone," wrote Renan, "and the masses of the human

* Joseph Comte de Maistre (1754-1821); French political philosopher who in his anti-revolutionary Christian-Catholic conservatism laid the groundwork of political "restoration."—*Translator.*

species, seeking enlightenment in the eyes of the thinker, demand to learn from him without equivocation whether *intrinsically the Truth is not sad.*"

On Sunday, November 30, of this year of grace —or disgrace—1924, I assisted at the Divine Office in the Greek Orthodox Church of St. Etienne, located nearby in the street named after Georges Bizet, and when I read the following sentence inscribed in Greek on the large painted statue of Christ which fills the tympanum: "I am the Way, the Truth, and the Life," I felt myself anew on an island, and I thought—or rather dreamed— that the Way and the Life might possibly not be the same as the Truth; that there might be some contradiction between Truth and Life; for the Truth can kill us, and Life can make us persist in error. And all this caused me to think of the agony of Christianity, the agony it carries within itself as well as the agony it suffers in each and every one of us. Or is it possible to conceive of Christianity apart from each and every one of us?

And here we are at the root of the tragedy. For Truth is something collective, social, and even public. We call "true" that upon which we can reach agreement and mutual understanding. Christianity, on the other hand, is something incommunicable. And this is the reason why it lies in agony in each and every one of us.

Agony (ἀγωνία) means struggle. The life of a

person in agony is one continuous struggle, a struggle even against life itself. And against death. This is the meaning of Santa Teresa's ejaculatory prayer, "I am dying because I cannot die."

What I am going to reveal to you, dear reader, is my own agony, my own strife for Christianity, the agony of Christianity within me, its death and resurrection at every moment of my inner life. . . .

In the religious sphere, and more especially in the sphere of the Christian religion, it is impossible to discuss questions of general, religious, universal interest without imparting to them personal or rather individual characteristics. Every Christian, in order to demonstrate his Christian existence, must of necessity say of himself: *Ecce Christianus,* as Pilate said: *"Ecce Homo!"* He must lay bare, as it were, his Christian soul, the soul which he has created for himself in the course of his struggle, his Christian agony. It is the goal of life to create for oneself a soul, an immortal soul, a soul which is the fruit of our own travail. For at the moment of death we leave to the earth a skeleton, and we bequeath a soul—our own creation—to history. This happens on condition that we have *lived,* that is, that we have joined battle with that kind of life which endures.

And Life? what is Life? This question implies even greater tragic possibilities than the question: what is Truth? For if the Truth cannot be defined because it is Truth itself which does the defining, it is at least equally impossible to define Life.

A French materialist—his name has slipped my mind—has stated that life is the sum total of those functions which resist death. This is a desperate or perhaps merely a polemic definition. Life, then, was for this man one prolonged struggle: it was agony. A struggle against death and also against the truth, against the truth of death.

People speak of the "struggle for life": but this struggle for life is life itself—*the* Life—and, in its totality, it is simultaneously the struggle itself—*the* Struggle.

What we shall have to meditate on is the real meaning of the Biblical legend as we read it in Genesis, where we are told that death came into the world through the sin of our first parents because they desired to be like gods, that is, immortal, by becoming knowers of good and evil, adepts of that science which imparts immortality. And, according to the same legend, the ensuing first death was a violent death, a murder: the murder of Abel, who was killed by his brother Cain—a fratricide.

Many people ask themselves how death comes to beasts of prey—lions, tigers, panthers, hippopotami, etc.—in the forests or deserts which are their habitats; whether they are killed or whether they die what is called a natural death, lying down in some corner, alone and in solitude like the greatest saints. And indeed in the manner of that greatest of all saints, the unknown saint— unknown above all to himself. Maybe he was born dead.

Life is a struggle, and the universal will-to-live is a struggle which manifests itself in struggle. I shall never get tired of repeating that what unites men most is their discords. And what unites each individual man with himself, what produces the innermost unity of our lives, is our inner discords, the internal dialectic of our discords. And, like Don Quixote, we never can make peace with ourselves except in dying.

Now if such is the nature of physical or corporeal life, the life of the psyche or the spirit is in its turn a struggle against eternal oblivion. And against history. For history, which is the unfolding of the thoughts of God upon this earth, lacks an ultimate human finality and is *en route* toward oblivion and unconsciousness. And all human effort tends toward giving to history a human finality; a supra-human finality, according to Nietzsche, who was the great dreamer of that ultimate absurdity: a social Christianity.

PREFACE TO THE
SPANISH EDITION OF 1930

This book was written in Paris, where I found
myself as an emigrant, having fled there at the
end of 1924, during the period of a full-blown
Pretorian and truly Caesarian dictatorship in
Spain. I was in an extraordinary state of mind, in
the grip of a sort of spiritual fever and night-
marish expectation: a state of mind which I tried
to describe in my book entitled, "How to Write
a Novel." And, as I indicated in the introduction
[to the French edition], the book presented here
[in Spanish] was written upon request.

Because I wrote originally with a view to the
book's being translated into French and to its
being destined for a large and predominantly
French audience, I was not particularly concerned with composing it for the appreciation and
taste of the Spanish-speaking public. I did moreover not anticipate that this book would ever—
as it now happens—be published in the Spanish
language. I entrusted my handwritten notes with
all the accumulated additions to the translator,

11

my intimate friend, Juan Cassou (who is as much a Spaniard as he is a Frenchman), and he transposed them into a vigorous French with a strong Spanish flavor—a feat which has without doubt contributed to the success of the book. There remains in the [French] text the pulse of that fever in which my notes were conceived. Later on, this short work was translated into German, Italian, and English. And now the time has at last arrived when it can appear in the language in which it was first composed.

Composed? One might object that this short work lacks properly speaking the rigor of composition. Maybe what it lacks is tectonic structure, but I do not believe that it lacks the truly vital elements of composition. I wrote it, as I said before, almost in a state of spiritual fever, reverting—in addition to the thoughts and sentiments which had preoccupied my mind for so many years—to those particular issues which were torturing me on account of the misfortunes of my country as well as those which chanced to come to my mind in the course of my present reading. A good deal of what is written here was dictated by the actual political realities as they prevailed in France at that time. And I did not wish to omit certain allusions which today—and in some distance from France—may appear to be of but little actuality and thus perhaps difficult to understand.

This short work recreates in a more concrete

and—because of its greater spontaneity—more intense and passionate form much of what I expounded in "The Tragic Sense of Life." And it gives me an opportunity to rethink certain ideas and to reshuffle them in my mind. This is what St. Lawrence is said to have done while he was suffering martyrdom in being roasted on a grid-iron.

Is this book a soliloquy? It is my so-called critics who have asserted that I write nothing but soliloquies. Maybe a better term would be mono-dialogues; or, better yet, auto-dialogues, that is, dialogues with my own self. And an auto-dialogue is not a monologue. The person who takes part in a dialogue, who converses with himself by dividing himself into two or three or more persons, or even into an entire people, does not soliloquize. Only dogmatists speak in mono-logues, even when they seem to engage in dialogues, by means of questions and answers, as is being done in catechisms. But we skeptics, we who are in agony, we polemical spirits do not soliloquize. As for myself, I carry my agony, my religious and secular struggle, too deeply in my spiritual entrails to be able to live on soliloquies. Job was a man of inner contradictions; so were Paul and Augustine and Pascal; and so I believe am I.

After this little book had been written and published in French, in February 1930, I believed that the time had come for me to return to my native Spain, and so I did return. I returned in order to resume here in the heart of my country my social or rather, properly understood, my political campaigns. And as I dug again deeply into these, I felt rising within me my ancient or, more correctly, my eternal religious anxieties, and in the heat of my political pronunciamentos I heard again a whispering voice which said: "And after all this, what next? And why?" And in order to silence that voice or the one who spoke to me through it, I continued to address the believers in progress, humanity, and justice and tried to convince myself of the excellence of these values.

I do not intend, however, to go on in this vein, although I am not afraid of being once again called a pessimist—a thing which causes me very little worry. I know only too well what has been wrought in the world of the spirit by that which simpletons and weaklings call pessimism, and I also know all that religion and politics owe to those who have sought consolation in conflict and struggle, even without any hope of eventual victory.

I do not wish to end this preface without calling attention to the fact that one of the things to which this slim book owes its gratifying success is that it has restored the true, original or etymological meaning of the word "agony" and the word "struggle." In consequence, people will henceforth not mistake a person in agony for a dying person or a person sick unto death. One can die without agony and one can live—and for many years at that—in and through agony. A person truly in agony is an "against"—sometimes a prot-agonist, sometimes an ant-agonist.

And now, dear reader [of the Spanish tongue], I bid you farewell, until we shall meet again in another auto-dialogue. Until then, I leave you to your agony, while I remain with mine, and may God bless them both!

1

AGONY

Agony, then, is struggle. And Christ came amongst us to bring us agony: struggle, not peace. He told us so Himself: "Do not imagine that I have come to bring peace to the earth; I have come to bring a sword, not peace. I have come to set a man apart from his father, and the daughter from her mother, and the daughter-in-law from her mother-in-law; a man's enemies shall be the people of his own house...... (Matth. 10:34-37). He remembered that the people of His own house, His mother and His brothers, thought he was mad, out of His mind, and that they went out to restrain Him (Mark 3:21). And on another occasion He said: "I have come to spread fire over the earth, and what better can I wish than that it should be kindled . . . ? Do you think that I have come to bring peace on the earth? No, I tell you, I have come to bring dissension; henceforth five living in the same house will be divided against one another, three against two and two against three; the father against his son and the son against his father; the daughter against her mother and the mother against her daughter; the mother-in-law against her daughter-in-law and the daughter-in-law against her mother-in-law" (Luke 12: 49-54).

"But what about peace?" we shall be asked. For it is of course possible to quote other and even more numerous passages in the Gospels which speak to us about peace. Yet the fact is that this kind of peace can grow only out of war, just as a certain kind of war can be won only in peace. And this precisely is agony.

Now someone might observe that peace is life —or death—and that war is death—or peace, for the manner in which these two are mutually assimilated is almost a matter of indifference: peace in war—or war in peace—is life in death, the life of death and the death of life: and this precisely is agony.

Is all this nothing but an intellectual fancy? If so, then St. Paul, St. Augustine and Pascal were some of the chief representatives of such fanciful thinking. The logic of passion is always imaginative, polemical and "agonistic." And the Gospels are filled with paradoxes, with burning bones.

And, like Christianity, Christ Himself is forever in agony.*

Terribly tragic are our crucifixes, our Spanish Christs. They are indicative of a Christ not dead, but in agony. A Christ already dead, already returned to the earth, already at peace, a Christ dead and buried by others who are themselves dead, that is the Christ of the Holy Sepulchre, Christ lying in His tomb; but a Christ Whom one adores on the Cross is a Christ in agony, a Christ Who cries out: *Consummatum est!* And it is to this Christ—the Christ Who exclaims: "My God, My God, why hast Thou forsaken me?" (Matth. 27:46)—to Whom believers in agony pay homage. And among these are many who believe that they have complete faith, who have faith in faith.

To live, to struggle, to fight for life and to live by struggle, by faith, that means to doubt. I have already affirmed this in another one of my books, where I called to mind that passage of the Gospel which reads: "I believe, help my unbelief!" (Mark 9:24). A faith which knows of no doubt is a dead faith.

And what does it mean: to doubt? The verb

---

* "Jesus will be in agony until the end of the world; we must not be asleep during this time." Thus wrote Pascal in "The Mystery of Jesus." And he wrote it in agony. For not to sleep means to dream while being awake; it means to dream in agony, that is, to be in agony.

dubitare contains the identical root—the root of the numeral adjective *duo, dos*—as the noun *duellum:* struggle. Doubt, Pascalian doubt, "agonic" or polemic doubt, is more than Cartesian or methodical doubt: it presupposes the duality of combat. I am speaking here of the doubt of Life (life = struggle), not of the doubt of the Way (way = method).

To believe what we do not see equals faith. So we have been taught in the catechism. To believe that which we do see—as well as that which we don't see—that is reason and science; and to believe that which we shall see—or shall not see— that is hope. And all this goes by the name of faith. I affirm, I believe, as a poet, as a creator, looking at the past, looking at memory. I deny, I disbelieve, as a rational being, as a citizen, looking at the present; and I doubt, I struggle, I am in agony, as a human being, as a Christian, contemplating the unrealizable future, contemplating eternity.

There exists in my Spanish fatherland, amongst my Spanish people—an "agonistic" and polemical people—a devotion to Christ in His agony; and there exists also a cult of the Virgin of Sorrows— the *Mater Dolorosa*—whose heart is pierced by seven swords. This is something quite different from the Italian *Pietà:* our people pay homage not so much to the Son Who lies dead in the lap of His Mother as they venerate the Virgin Mother herself, who suffers in agony, holding her Son in her arms. It is a cult of the Mother in agony.

People will tell you that there exists also a cult of the Infant Jesus, of the Infant holding the Globe in His hands, a cult of the Nativity, and a devotion to the Virgin who gives life, the Virgin who suckles her child.

I shall never forget as long as I live the spectacle I witnessed on the Feast of St. Bernard, in 1922, among the Trappists of Dueñas, not far from Palencia. The monks were chanting a solemn salute to Our Lady in the church dedicated to her, illumined with candles made from the wax of sexless bees. High above the main altar rose an image—of no great artistic value—of the Virgin Mother clothed in blue and white. She seemed to be depicted after her visit to her cousin, St. Elizabeth, and prior to the birth of the Messiah. With her arms outstretched toward heaven, she seemed to be anxious to fly heavenward with her sweet and tragic burden, the unknowing Word. The Trappists, young and old—some hardly of the age of fathers, others past that age—filled the church with the chant of their litany.

Janua caeli (Portal of Heaven), they sang, *ora pro nobis* (pray for us)! It was a cradle song, a lullaby in praise of death. Or rather in praise of not-being-born. They dreamed of re-living their lives, but in reverse, in the anxious desire to return to infancy, to the sweetness of childhood, so that they might feel on their lips the heavenly taste of their mother's milk and might once more enter into the shelter of the tranquil motherly womb to sleep in pre-natal slumber *per omnia saecula saeculorum* (for all eternity). And this wished-for state, which resembles so much the Buddhistic Nirvana—a truly monastic ideal—is also a form of agony, though on the surface it appears to be the very opposite.

In the Journal of Father Hyacinth—"Father" Hyacinth, let us not forget it—(of whom we shall have to say more later on)—we read under the date of July 9, 1873, the time at which he was expecting the birth of a child, an offspring of his mystical-carnal matrimonial union, the following statement concerning the immortality of the soul and the resurrection of the flesh: "May he rest in peace under his mother's heart, at least during those nine months of sweet slumber which are granted him!" The sweet dreamless slumber here referred to is that pre-natal earthly paradise of which the Trappist Fathers of Dueñas were dreaming.

In the book, *Os trabalhos de Jesús* by the Portuguese mystic, Fray Thome de Jesús, we are told about the labors which Our Lord Jesus Christ underwent during the nine months of enclosure in the womb of his mother.

The sufferings of the monks and nuns, the recluses of both sexes, are not caused by sexuality but rather by the problem of maternity and paternity, that is to say, by the problem of finality. They suffer because they know that their flesh, the carrier of the spirit, does not perpetuate itself, does not propagate itself. On the threshold of death, near the end of the world—the end of *their* world—they tremble in view of the desperate hope of the resurrection of the flesh.

The Trappists of Dueñas chanted: *Mater Creatoris, ora pro nobis!* Mother of the Creator! The human soul desires to create its Creator, Him Who is to eternalize it. Mater Creatoris! Mother of the Creator! This is a cry of anguish, a cry of agony.

The Virgin is called the Mother of God (Θεοτόκος, *deipara*). And the words, "Blessed is the fruit of thy womb" (Luke 1:42) are said of the Word by Whom all was made that has been made (John 1:3). Not only the soul but also the human body, which is destined to return to life, desires to create the Word, so that the Word may in turn create and eternalize the soul and the body —the cradle and tomb of the soul—the body from which the soul rises in birth and returns to a prenatal state, dies and rises again. To negate life is to die, and to negate death is to be born again. And this precisely is the dialectic of agony.

Perhaps one of those poor Trappists was praying for my conversion. And perhaps he was, without knowing it, also praying for his own conversion. In this manner Christianity manifests its agony.

But what is Christianity? For we are told that one must proceed by way of definition.

2

WHAT IS CHRISTIANITY?

Christianity must be defined "agonistically," polemically, in terms of struggle. Perhaps it is even more important to determine what Christianity is not. Christianity is certainly no "ism," no philosophic doctrine like Platonism, Aristotelianism, Cartesianism, Kantism, or Hegelianism. This glorious word rather denotes the quality of "being-a-Christian." As "humanity" denotes the quality of being-human, so "Christianity" has come to serve as designation for the Christian quality of a supposed community of Christians, a Christian society. But this is obviously an absurdity, since society kills Christianity, which is always an affair of solitary individuals. . . .

The true Christian makes himself another Christ. St. Paul knew this well: he experienced Christ being born, being in agony, and dying within himself.

St. Paul is the first great mystic, the first Chris-

tian in the proper sense of the term. Although the
Master appeared first to St. Peter (cf. Couchoud,
"On the Apocalypse of Paul," in *Le mystère de
Jésus,* chap. II), St. Paul saw Christ in himself;
He appeared to him, but St. Paul believed that He
had died and had been buried (1 Cor. 15:3-8).
And when Paul was taken up into the third heaven
and knew not whether he was in his body or out
of it, for God alone knows that—Santa Teresa
will repeat the same words many centuries later—
he was carried up into paradise and heard *unutterable words.* This is the only way we can translate the words ἄρρητα ῥήματα, which express the
antithetical style of "agonistic mysticism"—that
mystical agony which proceeds by way of antithe-
ses, paradoxes and even tragic plays upon words.
Mystical agony does play with words; it plays
with *the* Word. It plays with the creation of the
Word, as perhaps God played with the creation
of the world—not indeed to play with it after its
creation but playing in creating it, since creation
itself was a play. And once the world was created,
God handed it over to the disputes of men and to
the agonies of those religions which are perpetu-
ally in search of God. And in that elevation into
the third heaven, into paradise, St. Paul heard
"unutterable words," that is, words which cannot
be uttered by man (2 Cor. 12:4).

He who is incapable of understanding and
feeling this, of comprehending it in the biblical
sense, of rethinking and re-creating it in his own

mind, should despair of ever comprehending not only Christianity but also that which is anti-Christian, and even the meaning of history, of life, of reality, and of personality. Let him turn to what is commonly called politics—party politics—or to education, or let him dedicate himself to sociology or archaeology!

And so it is not only with respect to Christ but with respect to every human and divine power, with respect to every living and eternal human being whom one comprehends with a mystical knowledge, with an inward and mutually sympathetic understanding, where the knower and lover become the known and the beloved.

When Leon Chestov, for example, discusses the thinking of Pascal, he evidently fails to understand that to be a Pascalian thinker consists not in accepting Pascal's ideas but rather in being Pascal, in becoming another Pascal. As for myself, I have experienced it many times that, when I encountered in some piece of writing a human being rather than a philosopher, a sage, or a thinker, a soul rather than a doctrine, I told myself: "But this is the man I have been myself." Thus I have re-lived my life with Pascal in his century and environment; I have re-lived my life with Kierkegaard in Copenhagen, and I have had the same experience in many other instances. And is this not perhaps the most convincing proof of the immortality of the soul? Is it not true that these persons re-live their lives in me as I re-live my life in them? I shall know after my death whether or not I live again in others in this manner. Is it not true that even today some persons feel that they live in me, or that they live outside me, while at the same time I know that I do not live in them? And how much consolation there is in all of this! Leon Chestov says that Pascal "carries with him no solace, no consolation" and that "he annihilates every kind of consolation." Many believe this, and yet, what a mistake! For there is no greater solace than in being disconsolate, just as there is no more creative hope than the hope of those who are in despair.

We are told that human beings seek peace. But is this true? It is the same story when we are told that men seek freedom. No, the truth is that men seek peace in times of war and war in times of peace; they seek freedom when they smart under tyranny, and they seek tyranny when they live in freedom.

As to freedom and tyranny, we should not place so much emphasis on the saying, *homo homini lupus* (man is man's mortal enemy [literally, man is a wolf unto man]) but rather use the phrase, *homo homini agnus* (man is as a lamb unto man). It is not the tyrant who turns men into slaves; the reverse rather is true. There was a man who freely offered to carry his brother on his shoulders; it was thus not the latter who *forced* his brother to carry him. Man is essentially lazy, and with laziness is associated the horror of accepting responsibilities.

But let us return once more to the problem of mystical knowledge, and let us recall the saying of Spinoza, *Non ridere, non lugere, neque detestari, sed intelligere* (man should not laugh, nor lament, nor hate, but understand). *Intelligere:* understand? No, he should rather learn *to know* in the biblical sense of the term, that is, *to love . . . , sed amare!* Spinoza himself spoke of "intellectual love," but Spinoza was, like Kant, a bachelor, and perhaps he died in the state of virginity. Spinoza, Kant, and Pascal were celibate bachelors because they were not fathers; but they surely were not *monks* in the Christian sense of the term.

Christianity, or rather Christendom, from the time of its birth in St. Paul, was not a doctrine, although it expressed itself dialectically. It was a way of life, it was struggle, it was agony. The doctrine was the Gospel, the Glad Tiding. Christianity, Christendom, was a preparation for death and resurrection, for life eternal. "If Christ is not risen from the dead, then we are the most miserable of men," said St. Paul.

One can speak of "Father" Paul or "Father" St. Paul, for he was both an apostle and a holy Father; but it will not occur to anyone to speak of Father Spinoza or Father Kant. And one can speak—and should speak—of "father" Luther, the monk who got married; but again, one cannot speak of "Father" Nietzsche, although there are some people who think that Nietzsche's—the progressive paralytic's—*Beyond Good and Evil* is the equivalent of Luther's *sola fide* (salvation by *faith alone*), as the latter expounded it in *De servo arbitrio* (On the Enslaved Will).

Christianity was the cult of a God-Man, Who was born, suffered, was in agony, died and rose again from the dead in order to transmit His own agony to those who believed in Him. The passion of Christ was the center of the Christian cult. And the Eucharist, the symbol of His passion, is the body of the Christ Who dies and is buried in each and every one of those who are united with Him in Communion.

We must distinguish then, as we have repeatedly insisted, between Christianity (or rather Christendom) and "evangelism." For the Gospel is a doctrine indeed.

In what has been misnamed "primitive Christianity"—that is, in the kind of Christianity which preceded the death of Christ—in "evangelism"— there is perhaps contained another religion which is not Christian, a Judaic religion, which is strictly monotheistic and the foundation of theism.

This supposed primitive Christianity, the Christianity of Christ—and this is even more absurd than to speak of the Hegelianism of Hegel, for Hegel was Hegel and not a "Hegelian"—was, as has been reiterated a thousand times, apocalyptic.

Jesus of Nazareth believed in the impending end
of the world, and this is why He said: "Let the
dead bury their dead" and "My kingdom is not of
this world." He believed perhaps in the resurrection of the flesh, in Hebrew fashion, but not in the
immortality of the soul in the Platonic sense, and
He believed in His second coming into the world.
Proofs for these beliefs can be found in any hon-
est exegetical work, if we are permitted to assume
that exegesis and honesty are compatible.

And in this world-to-come, the kingdom of God,
the impending arrival of which was generally ex-
pected, the flesh would regenerate itself, would
perpetuate its seed, for death was destined to die.

The Gospel of St. Matthew (22:23-33) tells us
—in a passage which is of the very essence of
Christianity—that after the Pharisees had tempted
Jesus by asking Him whether or not one was obli-
gated to pay the poll-tax to Caesar, to the Empire,
He answered them: "Render to Caesar what is
Caesar's, and to God what is God's." And we are
further told that on that same day the Sadducees
—who, unlike the Pharisees, did not believe in the
resurrection of the flesh and in a life-to-come—
approached Him and posed this question to Him:
"Master," they said, "Moses told us: *If a man dies
and leaves no children behind, his brother shall
marry the widow and shall beget offspring in his
dead brother's name.* We once had amongst our
people seven brothers, of whom the first died after
having been married, and since he left behind

no offspring, he bequeathed his wife to one of his brothers. The same happened in the case of the second and the third brother, and in the end it happened to all of the seven brothers, and the woman died last of all. And now, when the dead rise again, which of the seven brothers will be the woman's husband, since she was wife to all of them?" And Jesus answered them, saying: "You are in error; you understand neither the Scriptures nor the power of God. For when the dead rise again, there will be no marrying and no begetting: they will be as the angels in heaven are. And in the matter of the resurrection of the dead, did you never read what God Himself said: *I am the God of Abraham, and the God of Isaac, and the God of Jacob?* He is not the God of the dead, but the God of the living. And this the multitude heard, and they were amazed by His teaching."

And thus the agony of Christianity follows its course, on one side the Pharisees, on the other the Sadducees.

But when Jesus died and Christ was reborn in the souls of all the faithful, to perpetuate His agony in them, then the belief in the resurrection of the flesh originated and with it the belief in the immortality of the soul. And that great dogma of the resurrection of the flesh (as the Hebrews understood it) and of the immortality of the soul (as the Greeks interpreted it) came to full fruition in the agony of St. Paul, a Hel-

lenized Jew, a Pharisee, who expressed it stam-
meringly in his powerful polemical Greek idiom.

Once the anguish in the face of the anticipated speedy end of the world had passed and
those who had listened to the words of Jesus,
and those who had received Him with palms
when He entered into Jerusalem, had seen with
their own eyes that the kingdom of God did not
arrive on this earth of the dead and the living, on
this earth of believers and unbelievers—"Thy
kingdom come!"—each of them envisaged for the
first time his own individual end of the world,
of the world which he himself was; for each of
them carried within himself the foreknowledge
of his own bodily death and of his personal
Christian existence, of his own personal religion.
Under pain of death each of them had to create
for himself a personal religion, a *religio quae non
re-ligat* (a religion which does not socially "bind
together")—a paradox. For as human beings we
live together, but each of us dies alone, and death
is the most extreme solitude.

Upon the disillusionment that came to the early
Christians with the realization that the world
would not come to a speedy end and that the
kingdom of God upon the earth was not just
around the corner, there followed the death of
history. This is assuming, of course, that these
early Christians, these "evangelical" Christians,
who listened to Jesus and followed Him, did pos-

sess a historical sense, a feeling for history. They may have been familiar with Isaiah and Jeremiah, but these prophets had nothing of the spirit of Tucydides.

P. L. Couchoud is correct when he says (in *Le Mystère de Jésus,* pp. 37 and 38) that the Gospel "does not pretend to be history, a chronicle, a factual narrative, a biographical document." It calls itself "Glad Tidings." And St. Paul calls it a *Mysterium* (Rom. 10:15-16). It is a Divine Revelation.

But this Divine Revelation, this mystery, was to become the Christians' history. History, however, means progress, change, and a revelation cannot progress, notwithstanding the fact that Count Joseph de Maistre speaks—with the dialectic of agony—of a "revelation of revelation."

The resurrection of the flesh, the Judaic, Pharisaic, psychical—almost carnal—hope came into conflict with the immortality of the soul, with the Hellenic, Platonic, pneumatic or spiritual hope. And this is the tragedy and the agony of St. Paul and of Christianity. For the resurrection of the flesh is something physiological, something wholly individual. A recluse, a monk, a hermit can rise in his flesh and live—if this can be called living —alone with God. But the immortality of the soul is something spiritual, something social. He who makes himself into a soul, he who creates a work, lives in and with his creation and also with his fellow-men: he is part of humanity, to the extent that humanity is alive. And this means he lives in history.

Nonetheless, the Pharisees, among whom the belief in the resurrection of the flesh originated, hopefully anticipated a social life, a historical life, a life as a people. For the true Deity of the Jews is not Jahweh, but the Jewish people itself. And the Sadducean rationalists regard the Messiah as the incarnation of the Jewish people, the Chosen People. They thus believe in their own immortality. This explains why the Jews are so much preoccupied with their physical propagation, with the numerical magnitude of their offspring, so that they may fill the earth with their children. It explains their preoccupation with the patriarchate, with the problem of race, with the progeny of their race. And this is why a Jew—Karl Marx—could claim to have created the philosophy of the protetariat (*prole* = race, offspring, progeny) and why he gave so much thought to the law of Malthus, who was a Protestant pastor. In other words, the Sadducean Jews, being materialists, were seeking the resurrection of the flesh in their children. And, of course, in money. . . . And St. Paul, the spiritualistic Pharisee, sought the resurrection of the flesh in Christ, not in a physiological but in a historical Christ—I am going to explain later what I mean by "historical," a term which refers to something that is not real but ideal—in the immortality of the Christian soul, in the immortality of history.

And this is why there is doubt—*dubium*—and struggle—*duellum*—and agony. The Epistles of St. Paul offer us the most sublime example of an "agonic" style. This style is not dialectical but agonic, for in Paul's Epistles there is no dialogue, but strife and polemic dispute.

3

WORD AND LETTER

"And the Word made Himself flesh and dwelled among us, and we saw His glory, glory such as belongs to the only-begotten Son of the Father." Thus we read in the Prologue of the Gospel according to John (1:14). And this Word, Who made Himself flesh, died after His passion, after His agony, and then the Word turned into the letter.

The flesh, we may say, turned into a skeleton; the Word became dogma, and the waters of heaven were washing the bones of the skeleton and were carrying their salt out into the sea. This was done by the exegesis of Protestant origin, the exegesis of the men of letters and of books. For the spirit, the breath, which is word and oral tradition, imparts life, but the letter, which is bookish, kills. And yet, the Apocalypse contains a mandate to eat a book. But he who eats a book dies without fail. The soul, on the other hand, breathes by the use of words.

"The Word made Himself flesh and dwelled among us. . . ." Here we meet with the often debated question, the "agonic" question *par excellence,* of the historical Christ.

What is the historical Christ? Everything depends on the manner in which one experiences and understands history. When I say, for example, as I have done repeatedly, that I am more certain of the historical reality of Don Quixote than of that of Cervantes, or that Hamlet, Macbeth, King Lear, and Othello created Shakespeare rather than that Shakespeare created them, people think that I am speaking in paradoxes; they believe that I am using a rhetorical figure of speech, whereas what I am trying to convey is the doctrine of an "agonic" insight.

First of all, a distinction should be made between the reality and the personality of the historical subject. The word reality is derived from *res* (thing), and the word personality is derived from *persona.* Karl Marx, the Sadducean Jew, believed that it is things which make and direct men, and this belief is the basis of his materialistic conception of history, of his historical materialism—which we might term realism. We, on the other hand, who want to believe that it is men, that is, persons, who make and direct things, nourish in ourselves, with doubt and agony, our faith in a historical, personal or spiritual conception of history.

Persona, in Latin, designated the actor in a tragedy or comedy, the one who played a part or rôle in it. Personality is the work which the person actualizes in history.

Which of these was the historical Socrates: the Socrates of Xenophon, that of Plato, or that of Aristophanes? The historical Socrates, the immortal Socrates, was not the man of flesh and bone and blood who lived in a certain epoch in Athens, but it was that Socrates who lived in each of those who listened to him, and out of all of these grew eventually the Socrates who gave his soul to humanity, and it is he who lives on in humanity.

Is this a sad doctrine? It is, without a doubt, for the truth is intrinsically sad! . . . "My soul is dying with sadness!" (Mark 15:34) It is difficult to understand that one has to turn to history to find consolation. The soul is dying with sadness, but it is the flesh which makes it sad. "Pitiable creature that I am! Who is to set me free from this mortal body?" (Rom. 7:24), exclaimed St. Paul.

And this body doomed to die is the carnal man, the physiological man, this human "thing," whereas that other man, who is alive in others, who lives in history, desires to live also in the flesh, desires to find roots for the immortality of the soul in the resurrection of the flesh. And this precisely was the agony of St. Paul. History is at least as much and perhaps more of a reality than nature. The person is a thing (*cosa*), for the word *cosa* derives etymologically from *causa* (cause). And even in narrating history we are making history. The personalist doctrines of Karl Marx, the Sadducean Jew, who believed that things are making men, have produced things. Among other things, they have produced the very real Russian revolution. Lenin was therefore much closer to historical reality when, in his reply to the reproach that he was at odds with reality, he said: "So much the worse for reality!" This shows how faithful a disciple of Hegel he was!

The Word-made-flesh desires to live in the flesh, and when death comes, it dreams of the resurrection of the flesh. "It was above all the idea of the Messiah and of the Blessed Age which He was to usher in that caused the idea of the unhappy fate which was to await those among the faithful who would die prior to its advent. To correct this injustice, one was willing to admit that they would rise again and even, in order to make for complete equality, that they would rise in the same body in which they had dwelled in this life. This is how that surprising dogma of the resurrection of the flesh originated, expressing a view quite opposed to the Greek conviction of the immortality of the soul" (M. Zielinski, *La Sibylle,* p. 46).

It was believed that the Word had risen from

the dead. Christ, the Word, spoke, but He did not write. There is one single passage in the Gospels—and it is for this reason thought to be apocryphal—at the beginning of chapter eight of the fourth Gospel, in which we are told that when the Pharisees presented to Jesus the woman taken in adultery, He bent down and wrote with His finger in the sand (John 8:6). He wrote with His bare finger, not with a cane or with ink, but in the sand on the ground, in letters which the wind would soon carry away.

But while the Word, the *Verbum*, did not write, St. Paul, the Hellenized Jew, the Platonically inspired Pharisee, did write or, more correctly, did dictate his Epistles. In St. Paul the Word turned into letters, the Gospel became a book—the Bible. And thus Protestantism began, and the tyranny of the letter begot St. Augustine, Calvin and Jansen. Maybe Keyserling was not far from the truth when he asserted that the living Christ would have found neither Paul nor Augustine nor Calvin among His followers.

It is necessary that we become fully aware of the principle of the intrinsic contradiction in religion. The Prologue of the fourth Gospel is the work of a man of books, a man of the letter, a biblical rather than an evangelical man. It starts out with the declaration that in the beginning was the Word, the *Verbum:* ἐν ἀρχή ἦν ὁ λόγος. He does not say ἐν ἀρχή ἦν ἡ γραφή (in the beginning was the written document, the letter, the book). Indeed: even in the embryonic evolution of the fleshly man the skeleton grows inward from the skin.

Thus there came into being the letter, the epistle, the book, and what was evangelical in the beginning became now biblical. And—the fountainhead of contradictions—the evangelical had expressed the hope for the end of history. And from this hope, which was vanquished by the death of the Messiah, there was born, in the midst of a Hellenized Judaism and a Platonized Pharisaism, the faith in the resurrection of the flesh.

The letter is dead; in it we cannot expect to find life. The Gospel according to Luke (24) relates that when the disciples, after the death of the Master, went to His tomb on Saturday and found the stone removed and the body of the Lord Jesus missing, to their amazement two men in shining white garments appeared to them, asking: "Why do you look for the living among corpses?" That is to say, Why do you seek the Word among bones? Bones do not speak.

The immortality of the soul, of that soul which manifests itself in writing, the immortality of the spirit of the letter, is a pagan philosophic dogma. A dogma of skeptics, and it is accompanied by a tragic query. It suffices to read Plato's *Phaedo* to become convinced of this. Perhaps these devout pagans nourished a dream of dying like the Trappists of Dueñas, a dream of being permitted to sleep forever in the Lord, or of being allowed to rest in the womb of Demeter, the Virgin Mother, of sleeping a dreamless sleep, of ending their lives like the men of the primeval Golden Age of whom Hesiod speaks (*The Labors and the Days*, 116), telling us that they died as if overcome by drowsiness: Θνῆσκον δ' ὥσθ' ὕπνῳ δεδμημένοι.

It was St. Paul, then, who turned the evangelical into the biblical, the Word into the letter. Now St. Paul is called the Apostle of the Gentiles. Apostle of the pagans? Pagan, the Latin *paganus*, means literally a man of the land (*pagus*), a villager, a peasant (*pagensianus*). And the peasant, the man of the fields—another contradiction—is a man of the word, not a man of the letter. The pagan in the proper sense of the term was an analphabet. Or is it not correct to say that the domain of the spoken letter is the countryside, and the domain of the written word is the city? We have but little faith in the *Volksgeist* of the German romanticists.

The analphabets, the unlettered, are usually those who are the most abject slaves of the *alpha* and *beta*, of the alphabet and the letter. A peasant's head is brimful with literature. His traditions are literary in their origin; they were first invented by some man of letters. The peasant is singing his folk songs to the accompaniment of liturgical music.

The Pauline religion—the religion of the letter

and perhaps also the religion of the written word —was a religion of the cities, of the urban masses, of the workingmen in the big social centers. It resembles in this respect Bolshevism, which likewise finds no entrance among the dwellers of the soil, the villagers, the Orthodox Russian "pagans" who adhere to the traditional spoken letter. What a world of contradictions!

Here, then, we are face to face with the agony of Christianity in St. Paul and in the Pauline religion which descends from him. Or, more correctly, which begot him. This was the tragedy of *Paulinitas:* the struggle between the resurrection of the flesh and the immortality of the soul, between the word and the letter, between the Gospel and the Bible. And the agony continues. "The thesis of the *Phaedo* is nothing but a subtlety. I much prefer the Judaeo-Christian system of the resurrection," wrote Renan (*Feuilles détachées,* p. 391). Read the *Choses passées* (things past) of the ex-Abbé Alfred Loisy, and you will witness a similar agony.

And simultaneously with the letter was born the dogma, that is, the authoritarian decree. And the struggle, the agony, was lodged inside the dogma and by force of the dogma itself, by virtue of the very contradiction which the dogma carries within itself, because the letter kills. And then followed the agony of dogmatism, the struggle against heresies, the struggle of ideas against thoughts. But the dogma continued to live on heresies, just as faith continues to live on doubt. The dogma maintained itself in existence by negations and it reaffirmed itself by negations.

Then came at last the greatest of all heresies—after Arianism, which now experienced a rebirth —the Reformation, initiated by Hus, Wiclef and Luther. I have heard it said that "after the Reformation had cut Europe in two, Christendom ceased to exist." And to this was added the statement: "Where, then, is mankind to be found for each and every human being? In his fatherland." This I read in a treatise entitled *La Déesse France* (The Goddess France [cf. Charles Maurras, *Enquête sur la monarchie, suivie d'une campagne royaliste au Figaro, et si le coup de force est possible*. Paris: Nouvelle Librairie Nationale, 1924]).

The Reformation, which was an explosion of the mentality of the letter, attempted to resurrect the Word in the letter; it tried to liberate the Word from the book, to draw the Gospel out of the shell of history, and it actually did bring into the open the ancient latent contradiction. And from then on agony became the very life of Christianity.

The Protestants, who established the sacrament of the Word—a sacrament which killed the Eucharist—chained the Word to the letter. And they set out to teach the peoples to read rather than to listen.

It is a curious thing—and it may be inserted

here as an amusing anecdotic digression—that the
mother tongue of Iñigo (Ignatius) of Loyola, the
founder of the Society of Jesus—which is the
same as the mother tongue of the Abbé Saint
Cyran of Port Royal and also the mother tongue
of my own parents and of all my ancestors—
namely, the *eusquera* or Basque tongue, became
a written language as a result of the Protestant
movement. The translation of the New Testament into Basque, the work of Juan de Liçar-
rague, a Franco-Basque Huguenot from Briscous
—the Basque Berascoya—was one of the earliest
books—perhaps the second book—written in
Basque.

The attempt was made to solidify the Word
with the aid of the letter, but the agony only
increased. Bossuet said quite aptly: "Since you
are changeable, you cannot be the truth!" But
back came the answer: "Since you are unchange-
able, you must be dead." And then the Church
and the Reformation began to battle against each
other as well as against and among themselves.
The outcome was that the Roman Church became more and more Protestant, and the reformed
churches became more and more Romanized. The
final result was that paganized and petrified
Christianity which prevailed in the Holy Roman
Empire, an Empire beset with the struggles between *Imperium* and *Sacerdotium*. And thus
came the end of the United States of the West,
and the era of national states began, the era of

the goddess France and the goddess Germany, the goddess England and the goddess Rome, and the poor sub-goddess Italy. Henceforth the so-called Christian citizens will be able to unite in the service of some patriotic, national or eco-nomico-social cause, but never again for an exclusively religious end. Spanish traditionalism will hoist its banner with the motto, "God, Fatherland and King," and Mazzini will cry, "God and the People!" But this God is no longer the God of Christ Who withdrew into the solitude of the mountain when the multitudes wanted to proclaim Him king.

During one of our recent civil wars in Spain and in my native Basque country (in the civil war of 1873-1876), the Carlist general Lizárraga —which was the name also of that Huguenot who translated the Gospels into Basque, and the name which my children bear from their mother's side—in his attack against the Liberals, flung heavenward this involuntary blasphemy: "Long live God!" It is quite in order to say: "God lives!" But imagine someone saying "Let God live!" in the subjunctive, desiderative and perhaps even imperative mood!

The Reformation attempted to return to life by way of the letter, and it ended by dissolving the letter; for free inquiry is the death of the letter!

4

ABISAG FROM SUNAM

The Third Book of Kings, chapter one, begins
with these words: "And now David the King had
grown old and was so far advanced in years
that it proved impossible to warm him, even by
heaping many coverlets on his bed. And so his
attendants said among themselves: Let us go and
find for our lord the king a young maid, so that
she may be brought to the court and that, by
sleeping near his heart, she may give warmth
to our lord the king. And they were looking in
all the lands of Israel for such a fair maid, and
they chose one and brought her to the king. She
was a very beautiful maid indeed, and she shared
the king's bed and waited upon him, but never
did the king mate with her."

Later we are told that Adonias, the son of Hag-
gith, rose up saying that he would reign after
David's death; and he assembled troops of par-

tisans. But the prophet Nathan said to Bethsabee, the mother of Solomon, that Solomon, not Adonias, was to succeed David. And he caused Bethsabee to go and see the great king, her companion in sin, in order to wrest from him the promise that Solomon, the child of sin, was to succeed to the throne, not Adonias, who already offered sacrifices and behaved like a king. The prophet Nathan aided Bethsabee in her efforts, and meanwhile Abisag, the great king's last spouse—and a virgin spouse at that—continued giving him warmth in his agony, unaware of the political conspiracy. And David promised Bethsabee with a solemn oath that Solomon was to succeed him on the throne.

"31. Bethsabee, bowing her face to the ground, offered reverence to the king, saying: May my lord, king David, live forever!"

Then David summoned the priest Sadoc, the prophet Nathan, and Banaias, the son of Joida, to his presence, so that they might anoint Solomon as king in Gihon, with the cry, "Long live king Solomon!" This they did, surrounded by a large crowd. And meanwhile poor Abisag of Sunam, unaware of these political machinations, continued to give warmth with her kisses and embraces to David in his agony.

Those who belonged to the party of Adonias— Jonathan, the son of the high priest Abiathar, and the others—dispersed. But Adonias, who greatly feared Solomon, rose, approached and clung to one of the horns of the altar. And then he offered reverence to Solomon the king.

The second chapter tells us of the counsels which David gave to Solomon, the son of his sin, when he was about to die. And then:

"10. David was laid to rest with his fathers, and he was buried in the House of David."

The biblical text does not tell us, but David must have died in the arms of Abisag the Sunamite, his last spouse, who with her kisses and embraces gave warmth to him in his agony; perhaps she rocked him into his last sleep with a motherly cradle song. For Abisag, the virgin, whom David did not "know" [carnally]—nor did she "know" David, except in desire—Abisag was the last mother of the great king.

And thus Solomon sat on the throne of David, his father, and Adonias, the rejected pretender, went to see Bethsabee and persuaded her to ask the new king to give Adonias as his wife Abisag of Sunam, the widow of David. Solomon was greatly annoyed when he became aware of the sly cunning of his elder brother, who in this manner tried to deprive him of his throne, and he swore to have him killed.

Solomon was the king of wisdom—and of voluptuosity—the king of shrewd politics, the king of great culture. But we have no further news of Abisag the Sunamite, who was languishing with love for her deceased great king David, the spouse of her virginity, whom she mourned with tears of fire and whom she wanted to bring back to life. Meanwhile Solomon reigned and kept a harem. Can you see the symbolic significance of this story?

David has always been for Christians one of the symbols, one of the types or prefigurations of Christ, the God-Man. The soul in love seeks to give Him warmth in His agony, in the agony of His old age, with the kisses and embraces of her flaming love. And since the soul cannot "know" her Beloved and—this is even more terrible— since the Beloved cannot "know" the soul, she despairs in her love for Him.

"To know" in the biblical sense is assimilated in meaning to the act of carnal—and spiritual— union, the act by which children of the flesh and children of the spirit are begotten. This meaning of the word "to know" merits some meditation.

Although in Genesis (1:28) Adam and Eve are commanded to grow and multiply—prior to their being forbidden under pain of death to taste the fruit of the tree of the knowledge of good and evil (2:17) which, according to the word of Satan, would make them like unto the Gods, a widespread popular Christian tradition has stubbornly persisted in understanding original sin— or what is commonly called the fall of our first parents in paradise—as carnal temptation. And with this sin and this fall began history and what we call progress.

'To know" means in effect to engender, and all vital knowledge in this sense presupposes a penetration, a fusion of the innermost being of the mind who knows and of the thing known. This is especially so when the thing known is, as is often the case, another mind or spirit, and even more when the thing known is God—God in Christ, or Christ in God. This is why the mystics speak of spiritual marriage and why mysticism is a sort of meta-erotic love, above and beyond ordinary love.

It should be emphasized that this kind of knowledge, that is, mystical or creative knowledge, is quite unlike rational knowledge, although no one can really say what the rationalists mean by the term reason! *Ratio* is one thing, and *Vernunft* is another. Leo Chestov, for example (who was a rationalist), has this to say with reference to Pascal: "The basic condition of human knowledge consists, I repeat, in the fact that the truth can be perceived by every normal human being." But what is meant here by a normal human being? Perhaps the mediocre "common man," the English "average man," the German *Durchschnittsmensch*? In other words, some fantastic entity: *Phantasia, non homo,* to use Petronius's expression (*Satyricon,* 38:16). And it is of these poor normal men who perceive nothing but rational truths that Count Joseph de Maistre—another "agonic" man—says somewhat arrogantly: "They possess nothing but their reason!" Nothing but poor human reason, no divine, creative truth.

Le pur enthousiasme est craint des faibles âmes
Qui ne sauraient porter son ardeur et son poids.

"Weak souls are afraid of pure enthusiasm; they would be incapable of bearing its fervor and its weight," sang Alfred de Vigny, another Pascalian man, in his *Maison du Berger* (House of the Shepherd). And let us not forget the precise meaning of "enthusiasm" (ἐνθουσιασμός, *endiosamiento*): The enthusiast is a divinely inspired man, a man who, being filled with God, is being transformed into God. And this is something which may happen to a poet, to a creative man, but it can never happen to a normal or average man.

Et n'être que poète est pour eux un affront.

"And to be only a poet is for them an affront." "They have nothing to offer but their poetry," exclaim our rationalists. The latter surely have to offer reason; and the poets have to offer poetry. But who offers truth?

Poor Abisag, the Sunamite woman, her soul filled with hunger and thirst for spiritual maternity, madly in love with the great dying king,

tried with wild kisses and embraces to keep him
alive, to revive him, to bring him back to life.
And she finally laid him to rest within her own
self. David in turn loved this poor girl, who gave
warmth to him in his agony, from the bottom of
his heart, but he was unable to "know" her. It
was a terrible fate for David and a terrible fate
for Abisag! For which of the two was it more
terrible? In other words, which is more terrible
for the soul, not to be able to love or not to be
able to be loved? Not to be able to know or not
to be able to be known? Not to be able to beget
or not to be able to be begotten? Not to be able
to impart life or not to be able to receive life?
Santa Teresa pitied the Devil because he is unable to love. And Goethe called Mephistopheles
the power which, in trying to do evil, is instrumental in producing the good; in trying to destroy, he builds. In other words, hate and even
more so envy are [errant] forms of love. The
genuine atheists are madly in love with God.

A great Spanish politician, Don Nicolás Sal-
merón, used to say that one loses the virginity of
faith in order to acquire the maternity of reason.
But there is such a thing as maternal virginity or
virginal maternity. And sometimes it happens that
virginity in the strict sense is lost without maternity—or paternity—being acquired, especially
when the blood is poisoned by some sin. And
there are certain eunuchs, like that Ethiopian

eunuch from Candace of whom we read in the
Acts of the Apostles (8:26-40) who succeed
in engendering a spiritual offspring.

The poor soul which hungers and thirsts for
immortality and for the resurrection of her flesh
—the soul which hungers and thirsts for God, for
the God-Man in the Christian or maybe in the
pagan sense of the term—consumes her maternal
virginity in kisses and embraces, in never-ending
agony.

In other books [of Scripture] you can read how
in Israel the people passed from a unified natural
cult (*monocultismo*) to the belief in one God
(*monoteismo*), and in still other books you can
find out what is meant by a God Who becomes
man or by a man who becomes God. At this time
I want to speak only of the nature of the inner
meta-erotic experience—a mystical experience, if
you want to call it that—and of the nature of
the agony of a soul which finds herself face to
face with the agony of her God—the agony of
love and of knowledge, of that knowledge which
is love, and of that love which is knowledge.

The soul which has given herself over to her
agony of love and of knowledge, renders hardly
any account to herself of Solomon's deeds, of his
political action, of history and of civilization;
nor of his Temple, the Church. If the soul pays
any attention to these matters at all, she does so
to rekindle her agony and because every soul
is a daughter of contradiction. But alas, Abisag

does not always have to rebuff Adonias. You may
well picture Abisag as the spouse of Adonias and
as the mother of his children, while Adonias is
warring against Solomon and while Abisag is still
in love with David. For there is only one great
love—the first is also the last and vice versa—
and in the soul of Abisag, the Sunamite woman,
her love for David was in conflict with her duty
toward Adonias, the son of David. What a
tragedy!

Will the embraces and kisses of Abisag accomplish the miracle of bringing David back
to life?

A miracle! Here we have one of the most con-
fused concepts, especially since belief in the
miracles of faith has nowadays been replaced by
faith in the miracles of science.

It has been said that "the savages are not overly
impressed by the prodigious applications of the
results of scientific discovery." It seems that when
a savage watches the flight of an airplane or
listens to a gramophone, he shows no great as-
tonishment. Quite naturally! He is used to watch-
ing the miracle of an eagle in flight, the miracle
of human speech or the miracle of a talking
parrot, and just one more miracle does not greatly
surprise him. For the savage lives surrounded
by miracles and mysteries. The primitive man,
who was born and has grown up in the midst of
people who call themselves civilized, never loses
his faith in miracles. If he does not believe in

the miracles of faith, he believes in the miracles of science.

On a certain occasion a convention dealing with astronomy was held in a well known public hall. The audience, consisting of men without scientific erudition, of employes of industrial firms and some manual laborers, showed themselves overawed when they heard the lecturer—that is, science—telling them about the many millions of miles which lie between the sun and Sirius. "But how was it ever possible to measure this distance?" they asked themselves, and then they added immediately: "Miracles of Science!" On the following day an expert tried to explain to these people how these distances are measured, and when they found out that aside from some complicated calculations the process is the same as that used by a land surveyor in measuring a piece of land or the method used in measuring the altitude of some mountain, they began to feel a profound contempt for science. There were among their number a few social mystics, some of those people who become actually inebriated with words when they speak of "scientific" socialism—the kind which has evidently reached its goal in the Bolshevik miracle!

It was Maurras who wrote (cf. *Enquête sur la monarchie*, p. 481): "I do not know what General André, who presumably is a positivist, thinks about this, but Auguste Comte. who was his teacher and mine, always believed that Catholicism was a necessary ally of science in the fight against anarchy and barbarism. He stated repeatedly that those who believe in God should become Catholics, while those who don't believe in God should become positivists. . . . He sent one of his disciples to the Gesú in Rome to enter into negotiations with the Jesuits. But some misunderstanding caused this project to founder; yet in bidding farewell to the Fathers, the delegate of Comte pronounced these grave words: 'When the political torments of the future will make manifest the full intensity of the modern crisis, you will find the young positivists ready to let themselves be killed for you as you are prepared to let yourselves be killed for your God.'

"Although Positivism and Catholicism are divided as far as the affairs of heaven are concerned, they are united in the affairs of this earth. M. Accard—'a Tainean Bonaldist'—whose image I find depicted in one of M. Paul Bourget's novels, is a positivist of a sort. . . .

"The Church and Positivism are both striving to strengthen the family. Both the Church and Positivism are inclined to sustain the political authorities as deriving from God or proceeding from the supreme laws of nature. The Church and Positivism are friends of tradition, of order, of the fatherland and of civilization. To sum it all up, the Church and Positivism have their common enemies. Moreover, there is not one French positivist who loses sight of the fact that if it was the dynasty of the Capetians which created France, it was the bishops and the clerics who were their first collaborators."

All this has to do with the kingdom of Solomon and with the dissensions between Solomon and Adonias; it has to do with Catholicism, but it has nothing to do with the rule of David and even less with his agony, with that agony which is the life of Christianity.

And what was the nature of the love of Abisag? Was it faith? Was it hope?

I have just been reading the words of the poet Paul Valéry (in *Variété*): "Hope is nothing but a distrust of being, regarding the precise foresights of the mind. This suggests that every conclusion that is unfavorable to being must be due to an error on the part of the mind" (*La crise de l'esprit*).

Auguste Comte demanded that "those who believe in God become Catholics," and Louis Veuillot, another one of the precursors of the *Action Française*, addressing the resourceful M. Henri Rochefort, had this to say: "My esteemed Count! It may be different with you who are so clever, but we little people need God or at least we need people who believe in God." But since Veuillot made a fine distinction between "having faith in God" (*croire en Dieu*) and "believing in God's existence" (*croire à Dieu*), a person like myself, not being a native Frenchman, finds it hard to understand what makes it necessary for people to have faith in God. And it seems we must despair of understanding the reason, since the same Veuillot asserts that "not everyone who wishes can learn French: one must have been born in France to be able to do this." And he adds: "French is a beautiful and noble language. And one does not know, speak and write French without possessing a goodly portion of those things which constitute what was formerly called 'a respectable man' (*l'honnête homme*). A Frenchman finds it difficult to live with a lie. To be able to speak French one must have in one's soul a fund of nobility and sincerity. You may contradict me by pointing to Voltaire. Voltaire—who by the way was no fool—spoke a language that was desiccated and already notably debased."

I am passing by Voltaire who, though certainly no Jesuit, was something worse, and I confine myself to the reassertion that I shall never understand the difference between "having faith in God" and "believing in the existence of God," nor will I ever understand what force compels those who believe in God to become Catholics. And as far as the problem of having oneself killed by the God of the Jesuits is concerned, this may well be a question to be decided on political grounds. Men are willing to have themselves killed for any idol. But there are few with a soul sufficiently strong to give warmth to their God in

His agony, few who will be capable of imparting life to Him so as to turn His very agony into life.

And this king David, whom Abisag wanted to revive with her kisses and embraces, this Christ in agony, will he make his Father, will he make God save us? It is in this latter context that we speak of "justification," which pertains to the realm of morality.

I have just been reading a passage in Leo Chestov's *La nuit de Gethsémani, essai sur la philosophie de Pascal* (The Night of Gethsemani, an Essay on the Philosophy of Pascal), where he speaks of the terrible dilemma with which Erasmus confronted Luther, namely: if our good works do not save us and if we can be saved alone by the grace of God which He—arbitrarily and freely—grants to some and refuses to others, "What then becomes of justice?" And Chestov has this to say: "Erasmus had no desire to discuss the Bible or St. Paul. Like all the world he condemned Pelagius and accepted St. Augustine's doctrine on grace, but he was unable to accept the monstrous idea that God is situated 'beyond good and evil,' that our 'free will,' our decision to submit to the Law be left to the highest tribunal; in short, that before God, man is deprived of any defense, even of the defense provided by justice. Thus wrote Erasmus, and thus thought and think almost all men—one might even say all men without exception." Yes, possibly all men, but surely not all Christians! And regarding the statement that God is situated "beyond good and evil," this is of course not so. "Beyond" (*jenseits*) is a Germanic word associated with Nietzsche, the "progressive" thinker. God is rather within good and evil, encompassing them, as eternity is within past and future, encompassing them, because eternity is *more* than time and only in this sense "beyond" time. And what about justice? It means something in morality; it means nothing in religion.

5

THE VIRILITY OF FAITH

Father Hyacinth, of whom we shall have to speak more at length, who, as a memory of his youth, had retained "the Catholic sadness of his family home, the suffering of his revered father and the melancholy soul of his good mother" (cf. Houtin, *Le Père Hyacinthe*, III, p. 250)—poor Father Hyacinth who had dreamed of finding the Church in the garden and in the cell of his monastery— entered into personal relations with Renan and on May 11, 1891 wrote to him as follows: "Is this an illusion? Is it only a memory, or is it still a hope? Please permit my simple and robust faith as a spiritualist and a Christian to hold on to this latter hypothesis. Besides, I accept so firmly the survival and final salvation of souls that I do not despair of being in full accord with you, if not in this world, then in the next" (Houtin, *Le Père Hyacinthe*, III, p. 370).

The simple and robust faith of Father Hyacinth did not understand that illusion, memory, and hope are not three hypotheses, but only one; that hope is a memory and that both hope and memory are illusions, and that faith is, according to St. Paul, "that which gives substance to our hopes" (Heb. 11:1). Paul says this of those things for which we hope as a result of an act of the will. But does not memory likewise depend on the will? The same St. Paul says with a Pindaresque overtone that eating, drinking, feasting as well as resting on the Sabbath day are "shadows of the future": σχιά τῶν μελλόντων (Col. 2:17). And memory is as much, if not more, a shadow of the future than hope is a shadow of the past.

In the "Journal" of Father Hyacinth we find the following entry under the date of October 18, 1892: "The thinker either affirms or denies. The intellectual power of Renan was unable to overcome doubt. He was lacking in virility."

He was lacking in virility! Virility is for this Father and monk—for him who wanted to be a father and to leave his carnal seed in this world of the resurrection of the dead—virility consists for him in overcoming doubt, in either affirmation or denial, in belief or disbelief. And to disbelieve is really to believe, because the saying, "I do not believe in the resurrection of the dead" can easily turn into the saying, "I believe that the dead will not rise again, that the dead remain dead." Thus faith becomes the daughter of virility; and affirmation or negation and dogma become the sons of virility.

Virility derives from *vir* (man), the male of the human species. And the same root underlies *virtus* (virtue), and faith, in the parlance of Christian theologians—though the terms theologian and Christian are in a sense contradictory—is a supernatural (*teologal*) virtue. It is not a "theological" virtue. There are no "theological" virtues unless they be perhaps embodied in that *furor theologicus* which begot the Inquisition!

But let us examine a little further this notion of virity, since our Father the monk seems to be of the opinion that to affirm or deny, to overcome doubt, is an "act of the will rather than an act of the intellectual power." Let us therefore examine the will and the will to believe.

William James, the pragmatist, another Christian in despair, another one of those in whom Christianity lies in agony, wrote an entire essay on "the will to believe." Has this will anything to do with virility? Is virility the source of the will?

Schopenhauer, who was of this opinion and who placed the focus of volition in the organs of virility, praised and admired us Spaniards because we imagine that this is actually so. In support of his opinion he cited certain popular and rather vulgar current expressions. Actually, the name of these organs never proceeds from the lips of those Spaniards who believe themselves men of will, of energy, of action. But one occasionally hears those horrible blasphemies where the sacred name, which should be hallowed, is grossly abused, as in that passage of Petronius's *Satyricon* where he speaks of a man who *putabat se colleum Jovis tenere* (II: 4 [who believed he had the organ of virility of Jupiter]). But is this *the will?*

The Spanish word *voluntad* (will) has no roots in the current and popular language. In French, *volonté* is close to *vouloir* (in Vulgar Latin: *volere;* in classical Latin: *velle*). But in Spanish we have no derivative of this Latin root. For *vouloir* we use the verb *querer,* which derives from the Latin *quarere* (to seek) and, deriving from *querer,* we have the noun *querencia,* which is used only when speaking of wild beasts, to designate the attachment they have for a certain place or person. That which in Spanish is thought to issue from the organs of virility is not will but desire (*la gana*).

Gana! An admirable word! *Gana* is probably a term of Germanic origin, notwithstanding the fact that Spanish is the most Latin among Latin languages, more so than Italian, which contains fewer Germanic elements. *Gana* denotes something like desire, turn of mind, appetitive striving. There are *ganas*—in the plural—of eating, of drinking, as well as *ganas* of trying to avoid oversaturation with food and drink. There are *ganas* of working and especially *ganas* of doing nothing at all. As someone expressed it: "The trouble is not that I don't feel any desire to work but rather that I feel such a strong desire not to work." And the *gana* to do nothing is called *desgana* (disgust). Virility marches forward toward its own destruction; it proceeds by way of solitude, by way of "eunuchism." This is what happens with those who voluntarily renounce all desire.

There is a justifiable and profound sense in speaking of spiritual voluptuosity—voluptuosity of the kind engaged in by a solitary onanist like the poor K. J. Huysmans, who was one more man in agony, at the time he was *en route* in search of Christian monastic faith, the faith of those solitary individuals who renounce carnal paternity.

"No me da la real gana! No me da la santisima gana" (To me is not given the royal desire, the most holy desire), exclaims a certain Spaniard. And on another occasion he says by way of euphemism: "This does not proceed from . . . virility." If it does not, whence does it proceed? What is the source of that royal and most holy desire?

Gana, as we have already stated, is not an intellectual power, and it may reach its fulfillment in *des-gana* (disgust). In place of *voluntad* (the will), it begets *noluntad* (the nil), derived from *nolle* (to will not). And *noluntad,* the daughter of *desgana*, leads to *nada* (the naught).

Nada is another Spanish word overflowing with life, pregnant with abysmal repercussions, a word which poor Amiel—yet another individual in agony (and how he did wrestle with the problem of virility!)—inscribes in Spanish in his *Journal intime. Nada!* That is the finality at which both the faith of virility and the virility of faith arrive.

Nada! Thus has come into being that special Spanish brand of nihilism—which might better be termed "nadism," to distinguish it from Russian nihilism—that is visible already in St. John of the Cross, that reappears in pale reflexion in Fénélon and Madame Guyon and that assumes the name "quietism" in Miguel de Molinos, the Arragonese Spaniard. This "nadism," which no one defined better than the painter Ignatius Zuloaga who said on the occasion he showed to a friend his portrait of the Wine Merchant of Segovia—a monster painted in the manner of Velasquez, a deformed and sentimental dwarf: "Ah, if you could only see what a philosopher we have here: he doesn't utter a word!" The important point is: the Wine Merchant did not say that there is nothing, or that all can be reduced to nothing: he simply said nothing! Perhaps this dwarf was one of those mystics submerged in the dark night of the spirit, of St. John of the Cross. And perhaps all the monsters of Velasquez are mystics of this type. Is not our Spanish art of painting truly the purest expression of our virile philosophy? The Wine Merchant of Segovia, by saying nothing about anything, has freed himself from the obligation to think; he is a genuine freethinker.

A faith of virility? There exists something

which we might call a craving (*ganas*) to believe rather than the will to believe, and this kind of appetite proceeds from the flesh which, according to the Apostle, lusts against the spirit (Gal 5:17). And this is so despite the fact that St. Paul speaks of the "will [appetite] of the flesh": Θελήματα τῆς σαρκός (Eph. 2:3); the flesh which turns sad after having sown its seed, while all the time creation groans in travail (Rom. 8:22). And nonetheless, the flesh must reproduce itself, and at the same time virility must be employed economically, so that sons of the spirit will be engendered. By which of these shall we be saved? By the children of the flesh through the resurrection of the flesh, or by the children of the spirit through the immortality of the soul? Are these two kinds of survival not in effect mutually contradictory?

Nonetheless, according to St. Bernard—a precursor of that naturalistic Franciscan piety which has such tender feelings for "brother pig," that is, the body—the flesh is a very good and loyal companion of the good spirit: *"bonus plane fidusque comes caro spiritui bono"* (cf. *De diligendo Deo* [*On the Love of God*], chapter XI). And is it necessary to remind ourselves of the *"mens sana in corpore sano"* (a healthy mind dwells in a healthy body) of Juvenal? But perhaps the perfectly healthy body contains a soul that is submerged in the naught like the soul of the Wine Merchant of Segovia.

A craving to believe! St. John of the Cross speaks of the "appetite for God" (cf. *The Ascent to Mount Carmel,* Book I, chapter X), and this very appetite for God, that is, when it is not induced by grace, "is of the same substance and nature as it would be if it were linked to matter and to a natural object: . . . it is merely natural and will remain so unless it be infused by God" (*The Living Flame of Love,* commentary to the fourth verse of the third stanza; cf. Jean Baruzzi, *Saint Jean de la Croix et le problème de l'expérience mystique.* Paris: Alcan, 1924, Book IV, chapter IV: "The appetite for God is not always an appetite inspired by God.").

The appetite is blind, says the mystic. But if it is blind, how can it believe, since believing is seeing? And if the appetite is unable to see, how can it affirm or deny?

"All that the world has to offer is either desire of the flesh or desires of the eye or the pride of life," we read in the first of the epistles attributed to the Apostle John (2:15-16). And to seek God in order to make sure that our flesh will rise again is as much a carnal desire as to seek Him in the world. If it is "agonic folly" to attempt the propagation of Christianity by means of the sword, by using the cross as a club, by means of Crusades, the wish to propagate Christianity by reproducing Christians carnally by means of the vegetative propaganda of carnal proselytizing is the same kind of folly.

The Crusade, too, is an expression of virility. It proceeds from arbitrary choice and not from grace. Crusades pertain to the most "agonic" acts of Christianity. The man who is trying to impose a faith upon another by means of the sword, seeks to convince himself rather than the other. He asks for visible signs; he hopes to perform a miracle in order to sustain his own faith. And every crusade which uses the sword ends with the victory of the conquered over the conqueror; and the conqueror turns into a nihilist (*nadista*).

It is necessary to economize with virility in celibacy, that is, in the state of active monachism. Honoré de Balzac, the author of *La Peau de Chagrin*, who has bequeathed to us so many children of the spirit—an entire populace of them—and, so far as we are able to ascertain, not a single child of the flesh, wrote an immortal page about celibacy in the context of a profound study of life in the Provinces, the life of craving desire: in the story of the *Curé de Tours*, toward the end of this psychological gem, we find those admirable lines describing the "*città dolente* (the town in sorrow) of the old maids," and the special concern of the author is the fate of Mademoiselle Salomon, who became a mother while remaining a virgin. We are confronted in particular with Hildebrand, that terrifying Pope—only a celibate can be infallible; only one who economizes with his carnal virility can impudently affirm or deny and thus pronounce the words,

"In the name of God I excommunicate you," while simultaneously thinking to himself: "God excommunicates you in *my* name; *anathema sit!*"

In the same context we hear of the "apparent egotism of those men who carry a science, a nation, or a set of laws in their bosom . . . in order to give birth to new nations or to produce new ideas." This is what Balzac calls "the maternity of the masses": maternity, not paternity. He also speaks of "giving birth" to (*enfanter*) rather than "engendering" new nations. And he adds that such men must combine in their powerful heads "the vitality of a woman's breasts with the force of God." This force of God is virility. But is God male or female? In Greek, the Holy Spirit is neuter, but He is identified with Santa Sophia, Holy Wisdom, which is feminine.

One must be economical with virility. But does this resolve the agony? *L'agonie* is the title of the last part of that "frightful philosophic study," as *La Peau de Chagrin* is called by its author. At the end of the novel, the protagonist—Rafael de Valentin, who more than anyone else struggles and suffers in agony—dies reposing on the body of Pauline, his wife, sinking his teeth into her breast, while Pauline says to Jonathas, the old servant: "What do you want? . . . It is I who have killed him. Have I not foretold you?"

We hope the reader is not unduly astounded that in this study on the agony of Christianity we have referred to two works of Honoré de

Balzac who, after all, was an evangelist and a Christian in his own fashion. But let us return to St. Paul.

The Apostle Paul did not "know" woman (I Cor. 7:1), and he recommended that those who are capable of doing so should abstain from such "knowledge." Thanks to such continence he was able to engender in Christ Jesus, by virtue of the Gospel (I Cor. 4:15), not indeed sons of the flesh, but sons of God (Rom. 9:8), sons of the free woman, not sons of the bondswoman (Gal. 4:23). To those who had wives he recommended that they should live as though they had none (I Cor. 7:29). But for the man who was weak, for the one who did not do the good he willed but the evil he did not will (Rom. 7:19)—the one who did not fulfill the will of the spirit that comes from God, but the desire of the flesh, the creature of the earth—he thought it better to get married than to burn with the heat of passion (I Cor. 7:9). Woman, then, is here regarded as a remedy for concupiscence.

A remedy for concupiscence! Poor woman! Yet woman will find her salvation in child-bearing (I Tim. 2:15), that is, unless she knows of something else she would rather do. For man does not stem from woman, but woman from man (I Cor. 11:9; Eph. 5:23), since Eve was made from a rib of Adam. Nonetheless, the Virgin Mother, of whom the virile Apostle of the Gentiles—as a matter of course—never speaks, was not born of a rib of Christ but rather He, Christ, was born of a woman (Gal. 4:4).

Christ was born of a woman—even the historical Christ, He Who returned to life from the dead. Paul tells us that it was Peter by whom the risen Christ was first seen; he does not say that Peter saw Him but—in the passive—that Christ was seen by Peter; and the last by whom He was seen was Paul himself, "the least among the Apostles" (I Cor. 15:9). But the fourth Gospel, the one which might be called the feminine Gospel, tells us that the first person to whom the risen Christ appeared was a woman—Mary Magdalene—not a man (John 20:15-17). Thus Christ was seen by Peter and heard by the Magdalene. When He appeared to Magdalene in a spiritual body, as a vision, she did not recognize Him until, having heard Him say lovingly, "Mary," she responded: "Rabboni," that is, "Master!" And Christ, Who was not a mere apparition—that is, a mere silent image—but the Word, the Logos, spoke to her. And Jesus said to the Magdalene: "Do not touch Me!" The person who thought it necessary to touch in order to be able to believe was a man—Thomas. For him it was necessary to see the signs of the nails in the hands of Jesus and to touch them with his finger: to see by means of the sense of touch. And to him Jesus said: "If you had not seen Me, you would not have believed. Blessed are those who believe without having seen" (John 20:24-30). This is why it is said that faith consists in believing what one has not seen, but heard. And Christ, after having said to Magdalene, "Do not touch Me," continued: "I have not yet gone up to My Father. Go and seek My brethren and tell them that I am going up to Him Who is My Father and your Father, Who is My God and your God." And Mary went forth to tell what she had seen and especially what she had heard.

The letter is seen, but the word is heard, and faith enters through hearing. Paul himself, when he was taken up to the heavens, heard "unspeakable words." The Samaritan woman heard Christ, and Sarah, already an old woman, had a son by virtue of faith; and Rahab, the harlot, was saved by her faith (Heb. 11:11-31). What more proof is needed? It was not a woman, but an eunuch— the Ethiopian eunuch of Candace—who had been reading Isaias and came to believe because of the words he had heard from the mouth of the Apostle Philip (Acts 8:26-40).

Faith is passive, feminine, the daughter of grace; not active, masculine, and a product of arbitrary choice. The beatific vision is a good reserved for the life to come. But is it a vision or an audition? Faith here below is a gift from Christ, the Christ Who rises from the dead; it is not of the flesh (Rom. 10:7). It is given by that Christ Who had a virginal body, and the members of Whose body are the Christians (I Cor.

6:15), according to the polemical phraseology of Paul.

Pagan mythology presents to us a man, a male god who, without the labor of woman, begets a daughter: Jupiter begets Minerva; she springs from his head.

What, then, about faith? A truly living faith— a faith which thrives on doubt and never "overcomes" doubt, the faith of a Renan—is a will to know that is being transformed into a will to love; a will to comprehend which is being transformed into a comprehension of the will; it is *not* a craving desire (*unas ganas*) which, via virility, ends in the naught. And all the while such a faith is in a state of agony, in a state of strife.

Virility, will, craving desire is one thing; another is faith, femininity, woman, and the Virgin Mary; she who is also the Mother of Faith: mother of faith by virginity.

"I do believe; Lord, help my unbelief!" (Mark 9:24). "I believe" here means: "I want to believe," or better: "I have a craving desire to believe," and as such the saying expresses the force of virility, the power of arbitrary choice (*liberum arbitrium*), which is precisely what Luther called *servum arbitrium* (a will in bondage). "Help my unbelief!" expresses the strength of femininity, which is the power of grace. And faith, notwithstanding Father Hyacinth's opinion to the contrary, issues from grace and not from arbitrary

choice. He who has merely a craving for faith
does not have faith. Mere virility is sterile. The
Christian religion, on the other hand, has conceived of the idea of pure maternity, without the
aid of man—the faith of pure grace, of efficacious
grace.

The faith of pure grace! The angel of the Lord
entered the room of Mary and, extending his
greeting to her, said: "Do not be afraid, Mary;
you have found favor in the sight of God"; and
he announced to her the mystery of the birth of
Christ. And Mary asked him how this could be,
since she had no knowledge of man. And the
angel explained it to her. And then Mary said:
"Behold the handmaid of the Lord; let it be done
unto me according to your word." And the angel
left her (Luke 1:26-39).

Full of grace (Κεχαριτωμένη): one woman only
is called by this title (Luke 1:28), the symbol of
pure femininity, of virginal maternity. This
woman had to "overcome" no doubts, for she had
none; nor had she need of virility. "Blessed are
the poor in spirit, for theirs is the kingdom of
heaven! Blessed are the pure of heart, for they
shall see God!" (Matth. 5:3 and 8).

The name of "Threads of the Virgin" is applied
to certain tiny threads that float in the wind and
on which a certain kind of spiders—which Hesiod
(cf. *The Labors and the Days*, 777) calls flying
spiders—take flight in the free breezes of the air
and even in the midst of a violent storm. There

are also such things as winged seeds, equipped with tufts. But these spiders spin those floating threads out of their own entrails, delicate webs by means of which they hurl themselves into space unknown. What an awesome symbol of faith! For faith hangs on the threads of the Virgin.

It is said that when the scorpion finds himself surrounded by flames and in danger of perishing in the fire, he thrusts his poisonous sting into his own head. Is not our kind of Christianity and our kind of civilization self-destructive in the same manner?

The Apostle says of the polemic of agony that he who fights, he who is in agony, is victorious over everything: πᾶς δὲ ὁ ἀγωνιζόμενος πάντα ἐγκρατεύεται (1 Cor. 9:25). Paul himself, too, fought his good fight, lived his good agony: τὸν καλὸν ἀγῶνα ἠγώνισμαι (2 Tim. 4:7). Was he victorious? In this kind of battle, to vanquish is to be vanquished. The triumph of agony is death, and this kind of death is perhaps eternal life. "Thy will be done, on earth as it is in heaven"; and "Let it be done unto me according to Thy word." The act of generation, too, entails an agony.

6

THE PRETENSE OF
SOCIAL CHRISTIANITY

What is all this talk about social Christianity?
What is all this noise about the social kingdom
of Christ with which the Jesuits din our ears?
What business has Christianity, true Christianity,
with our this-wordly society? And what about the
much heralded Christian democracy?

"My kingdom is not of this world" (John
18:36), said Christ when He saw that the end
of history was not at hand. And again: "Give to
Caesar what is Caesar's, and to God what is
God's" (Luke 20:25). But we must remember in
what circumstances this sentence of cardinal im-
portance was pronounced.

Those who persecuted Christ in order to destroy Him agreed among themselves to ask Him
whether it was lawful to pay tribute to Caesar,
the invader, the enemy of the Jewish fatherland,

who represented the political authority. If He answered in the affirmative, they would then picture Him to the people as a bad Jew, as a bad patriot; and if He answered in the negative, they would accuse Him of sedition in the face of the imperial authorities. Once the question had been posed, Jesus asked for a piece of money and, pointing to the image depicted on the coin, He inquired: "Whose picture is this?" "Caesar's," they replied. And then He said: "Very well: give to Caesar what is Caesar's, and to God what is God's." The meaning is clear: give to Caesar, to the world, to society the money which belongs to Caesar, to the world, to society; and to God give the soul which is destined to rise with its body. Christ thus detached Himself from every problem of social economy; the same Christ Who said that it is more difficult for a rich man to enter into the kingdom of heaven than for a camel to pass through the eye of a needle; and He showed clearly that His glad tidings have nothing to do with socio-economical or national questions, nothing with democracy or international demagogy, nothing with nationalism.

In the fourth Gospel we are told the reason why the Scribes and Pharisees condemned Christ —or rather the pretext: He was not a patriot! "So the chief priests and Pharisees gathered in a council meeting and said: What are we going to do? This man is performing many miracles, and if we allow him to go on like this, all will believe in him, and the Romans will come and will make an end of our city and our race." And one of them, Caiphas, who held the office of High Priest in that year, said to them: "You have no perception at all; you do not realize that it is best that one man be put to death for the sake of the people, so that the whole nation may be safe from destruction" (John 11:47-51).

We can see thus clearly that they sought to destroy Him because of His anti-patriotism, because His kingdom was not of this world, because He was not preoccupied with political economy, nor with democracy, nor with patriotism.

But after Constantine, after the beginning of the Romanization of Christendom, when the desire began to grow to change the letter—not the word—of the Gospel into something resembling one of the laws of the Twelve Tables,(*) the Caesars went to work trying to protect the Father from the Son, and God from Christ and from Christendom. And thus came into being that horrible thing known as Canon Law. Thus the juridicial, mundane and social conception of so-called Christianity was consolidated. St. Augustine, the man of the letter, was already a jurist, a legalist. So was St. Paul, who was simultaneously a mystic—a man in whom the mystic and the jurist were at war. On one side stood the law, on the other side grace.

* In Roman antiquity, the *Twelve Tables* contained the body of Roman Law as drawn up by the Decemvirs in 451 B.C.—*Translator*.

Law and duty are juridicial rather than religious and Christian concepts. Christianity is essentially grace and sacrifice. And what is called Christian democracy is something like "blue chemistry." The man who tolerates tyranny can be as much a Christian as the one who defends democracy or civil liberty. The fact is that the Christian qua Christian is not concerned with all this.

But since the Christian is a member of society, a civic being, a citizen, how can he be disinterested in social and civic life? Alas, the fact is that Christianity demands absolute solitude; the fact is that the ideal of the Christian life is the life of a Carthusian who leaves father and mother and brothers for the sake of Christ, who renounces the wish to become a family man, a married man and a father. But this ideal is impossible of fulfillment if the human race is to survive, if Christendom in the sense of a social and civic community of Christians is to survive, if the Church itself is to survive! And herein consists the real terror of the agony of Christianity.

It is impossible to actualize in history that which is anti-historical, that which is the negation of history—whether it be the resurrection of the flesh, or the immortality of the soul, the word or the letter, the Gospel or the Bible. To live historically means to bury the dead in order to be able to live by their death. It is the dead who rule over us in history, and the God of Christ is not a God of the dead but a God of the living.

Pure Christianity, evangelical Christianity, wants to seek eternal life outside history, but it encounters only that eternal silence which frightened Pascal, whose life was one Christian agony! And meanwhile history remains the thought of God upon this earth of men.

The Jesuits, the decadent sons of Iñigo of Loyola, are singing to us the balladesque refrain of the social kingdom of Jesus Christ, and with this concept as their standard of measurement they are trying to deal with political and socio-economical problems. On this basis, for example, they defend private property. But Christ is not interested either in socialism or in private property. And by the same token the side of the Divine anti-patriot, which was pierced by the lance and from which blood and water poured forth—an event which caused a blind soldier to see and believe—has nothing to do with the "Sacred Heart" of the Jesuits. The soldier was blind, without a doubt, and he saw as soon as he was touched by the blood of Him Who said that His kingdom was not of this world.

And then take a look at those other poor devils—devil (*diabolos*) means antagonist, enemy —who say that Jesus was a great democrat, a great revolutionary or a great republican! The passion of Christ is still in progress. For it is a great and terrible passion which He has to endure: some trying to make of Him a radical socialist, others a block-nationalist; some wanting to see in Him a Freemason and still others a Jesuit! But in the eyes of the High Priests, the Scribes and the Pharisees He was simply an anti-patriotic Jew.

"There is surely a great temptation for a priest who abandons the Church to become a democrat. . . . This was the fate of Lamennais. It was a sign of great prudence on the part of Abbé Loyson to have resisted all temptations in this respect and to have turned his back on all those expressions of endearment which the party of progress never fails to show to those who are breaking their official ties." Thus speaks Renan (cf. *Souvenirs d'enfance et de jeunesse*, p. 195). But Abbé Loyson—better known as Father Hyacinth—got married, founded a family, had children and became a citizen; and, seeing himself reproduced in the flesh of others, he did not have to wait for his own resurrection and was bound to experience within himself the birth of an ardent desire to achieve immortality in history; and thus he became of necessity preoccupied with social problems.*

Let us not forget—and let this be said with

* Abbé Loyson (Père Hyacinthe, O.C.), 1827-1912, was at first a Dominican priest, became a Carmelite in 1862, and from 1864 to 1869 was a celebrated preacher in Paris. He abandoned Roman Catholicism and joined the "Old Catholic Church" in Geneva (1873-1874); in 1879 he founded the *Eglise catholique-gallicane* in Paris.—*Translator.*

all due reverence—that Christ was a celibate and that for this if for no other reason He was bound to appear as anti-patriotic to His biblical compatriots. No, three time no: democracy, civil liberty or, on the other side, dictatorship and tyranny have as little to do with Christianity as has science. The social work of Belgian Catholicism, for example, has as little to do with Christianity as has Pasteur. It is not the mission of Christianity to solve the problems of social economy, the problem of poverty and wealth, the problem of the distribution of earthly goods. And this remains true despite the fact that he who redeems the poor man from his poverty also redeems the rich man from his riches, and that he who redeems the slave also redeems the tyrant; and that the death penalty should be abolished not only in order to save the condemned man but in order to save the hangman. And yet all this is not the mission of Christianity. Christ calls the poor and the rich, the slaves and the tyrants, the condemned men and the executioners. What, after all, do poverty and riches, slavery and tyranny, being executed or being the executioner amount to in the face of the impending end of the world, in the face of death?

"The poor you will always have with you," said Christ. Not, as some of those who call themselves social Christians seem to believe, so as to be able to practice almsgiving, to practice what they call charity, but because there will always be a civil society, there will always be fathers and children, and because poverty is an integral part of civil society and of civilization.

When in Spain a beggar asks for an alms for the sake of the love of God and the alms is not given him, it is customary to say to the poor man: "Forgive me, brother, for God's sake!" And since the beggar has been asking for something "for God's sake" (*por Dios*), he is called a *pordiosero*. And since the other man, who is supposedly wealthy, asks the beggar's forgiveness "for God's sake," one might call him too a *pordiosero*. Thus both of them are beggars for God's sake (*pordioseros*).

On May 13, 1901, Father Hyacinth wrote in Jerusalem: "Madame Yakovlev, the wife of the Russian Consul in Jerusalem, deplores, as do we, that the Christian churches have made of Jerusalem a city of ignorance, filth, sloth, and mendacity. It will be this way wherever the priests exercise their rule. Take Zola's *Lourdes* as an example. Madame Yakovlev says that we have calumniated the ancient Greeks and Romans. They had the idea of one God, and their statues were nothing but symbols. Nor were their manners and customs more corrupt than are those of today, while their dignity of character and the dignity of their lives were greater. What then is it that constitutes the great novelty of Christianity?"

Christianity has certainly not done away with

ignorance and filth, nor has it introduced dignity into human character and human life, at least not what men of the world call dignity.

A Spanish priest, Jaime Balmes, wrote a book entitled "A Comparison between Protestantism and Catholicism with respect to their Relationship to Civilization." Well and good: it is quite possible to evaluate Protestantism and Catholicism in their respective relationship with civilization; but Christianity, evangelical Christianity, is not concerned with civilization; nor with culture. Neither with Latin culture (written with a small *c* with a soft curve and well rounded) nor with German *Kultur* (written with a capital *K* and four pointed spikes like those of a *cheval-de-frise*).*

And since without civilization and culture Christianity cannot live, it lies in perpetual agony. So does Christian civilization, which as such is an intrinsic contradiction in terms. And Christianity as well as the civilization which we call Graeco-Roman and Western live by virtue of this agony: the death of the one would mean the death of the other. If Christian faith—that despairing and agonic faith—were to die, our civiliza-

* Plural: *Chevaux-de-frise:* "Frisian horses" are pieces of timber traversed with wooden spikes, pointed with iron; five or six feet long. They were used in warfare to defend a passage or as obstacles to ward off an attack. They are said to have been first employed at the siege of Groningen in Friesland.— *Translator.*

tion would also die; and if our civilization dies, so does Christian faith. And thus it is that we are destined to live in agony.

The pagan religions were state-religions and as such politically oriented; Christianity, on the other hand, is a-political. But from the time it became Catholic, and Roman to boot, it became pagan by turning into a state religion; it thus became political—it even included a Papal State! And its agony increased.

Is Christianity pacifist? This, it seems to me, is a meaningless question. Christianity is above, or if you will, below secular and purely moral— or perhaps merely political—distinctions, such as pacifism and bellicosity, civism and militarism; above such slogans as *"si vis pacem, para bellum"* (if you desire peace, prepare for war), which may easily turn into *"si vis bellum, para pacem"* (if you desire war, prepare for peace): prepare yourself for war in times of peace.

We have already referred to Christ's saying that He had come to bring dissension into families, to bring fire (πῦρ), division (διαμερισμόν), and a sword (μάχαιραν [Matth. 10:34]). But when on the Mount of Olives He was surprised by those who had come to seize Him, and when His disciples asked Him whether they should defend themselves with their swords, He answered them that they should let them have their way *on this occasion*, and He even healed the one whose ear had been wounded (Luke 22:50-52). And Peter, who had drawn his sword and had wounded Malchus, one of the servants of the High Priest, He reprimanded and said to him: "Put your sword into its scabbard, for all those who take up the sword will perish by the sword!" (Matth. 26: 51:53; John 18:2).

The fourth Gospel, the one named after John, is the only one which tells us that the disciple who drew his sword to defend with it the Master, was Simon Peter, the rock upon which the Catholic Apostolic Roman Church is supposedly built, the presumed founder of that dynasty which established the secular power of the Popes and preached the Crusades.

The fourth Gospel is considered the least historical in the materialistic or realistic understanding of the meaning of history; but in a deeper sense, in the idealistic and personal sense, the fourth Gospel, the symbolic Gospel, is much more historical than the three synoptic Gospels. It records and transmits much more authentically the agonic history of Christianity.

And in this Gospel—which is the most historical because of its being at once the most symbolical and the most vital of the four Gospels—the symbolic founder of the Pontifical Roman Catholic dynasty is told that he who draws the sword will perish by the sword. In September, 1870, the troops of Victor Emmanuel of Savoy entered the Rome of the Papacy by force of the sword. And the agony of Catholicism, which began on the day on which the Vatican Council proclaimed the Jesuitic dogma of papal infallibility, was now intensified.

Here we have a truly militaristic dogma, a dogma born in the heart of a militia, a company founded by an ancient soldier, a military man who, after having been wounded and rendered useless for the ranks of the militia of the sword, founded the militia of the Crucifix. He did so inside the Roman Church, establishing that discipline (*discipulina*) by means of which the disciple (*discipulus*) does not learn—*non discit*—but receives passively the order and the dogma. The dogma, not the *doctrine* of the master, but the *order* of the chief, who is placed above the master, in accordance with that third degree of obedience which Loyola recommended to the Fathers and Brothers of the Portuguese Province. And this surely is agony!

May we then expect the Roman Church to preach peace? A short time ago, the Spanish bishops in a collective document proclaimed a war for the civil protectorate (!) which the Kingdom of Spain—not the Spanish nation—wants to establish in Morocco. The bishops called this war a *Crusade!* And this name refers not so much to the cross which the warriors wear as an emblem as it does to that cross which these same warriors wield like a club and with which they are going to crush the heads of the infidels! Truly a terrible agony!

Thus, if the Catholic Church wants to remain Christian, it cannot afford to preach either war or peace. Louis Veuillot says: "We believe that it is less difficult to repair the ruins of war than to repair the ruins of peace. It is easier to reconstruct a bridge, to rebuild a house, to replant an orchard than to tear down a brothel. As far as humans are concerned, this thing proliferates on its own, and war kills fewer souls than peace. There is not a single positive article against war in the *Syllabus.** It is peace more than anything else that is responsible for the war waged against God" (cf. *L'Univers,* June 26, 1869).

It is almost inconceivable to put in writing a greater number of blasphemies. Would this same man have written these words after [the battle of] Sedan? Would he write them today, in the year 1925? Perhaps he would, for this kind never recognize their own errors. At any rate, war certainly is responsible for a larger number of brothels than peace, and it is by no means certain

* Reference is made here to the *Syllabus* promulgated by Pope Pius IX on December 8, 1864. It lists specifically and condemns a large number of doctrines and practices in nineteenth century political and social life as well as in intellectual life and in education (e.g., Socialism, Communism, Liberalism, Rationalism, Naturalism).—Louis Veuillot (1813-1883) was one of the leading French polemical writers of the nineteenth century. In his books and as editor of *L'Univers* he defended the rights of Roman Catholicism and of the Papacy.—*Translator.*

that "this thing" (viz., human kind) proliferates on its own, nor that war kills fewer souls than peace. War saddens and darkens the soul. And peace may do the same. There is possibly no positive article against war in the *Syllabus,* but there surely are positive articles against war and against peace, as well as for war and for peace, in the Gospels. For war and peace are things of this world, which is not the kingdom of Christ. Abisag, the Sunamite, had nothing to do with the works of Solomonic peace nor with the war between Solomon and Adonias.

The struggle of Christianity, its agony, pertains neither to the peace nor to the wars of this world. And it is meaningless to ask whether mysticism is active or contemplative, since it is active contemplation and contemplative action.

Nietzsche spoke of that which is beyond good and evil. Christianity is beyond war and peace. Or, rather, it is situated strictly apart from both war and peace.

The Roman Church, or rather the Church of the Jesuits, preaches peace of a sort: the peace of conscience, of implicit faith, of passive submission. Leo Chestov (in "The Night of Gethsemani") says very aptly: "Let us remember that the earthly keys of the kingdom of the heavens were suited for St. Peter and his successors precisely because Peter knew how to sleep and actually did sleep while God, Who had descended from heaven and dwelled amongst men, prepared

Himself to die on the cross." St. Peter knew how to sleep and actually did sleep without being aware of it. And St. Peter was the Apostle who denied the Master until he was awakened by the cock, the cock who awakens all sleepers.

7

ABSOLUTE INDIVIDUALISM

With regard to all these questions we are told that Christianity and Western or Graeco-Roman Civilization will disappear jointly and that, by way of Russia and of Bolshevism, another civilization will arrive, a civilization which—by whatever name we may call it—will be Asiatic, Eastern, Communistic, and ultimately rooted in Buddhism. For Christianity is an expression of radical individualism. But nonetheless, the real father of Russian nihilism is Dostoevsky, a despairing Christian, a Christian in agony.

But here we meet head-on with the fact that there are no more intrinsically contradictory concepts—concepts which lend themselves more easily to contradictory applications—than those of individualism and communism as well as those of anarchism and socialism. It is absolutely impossible to clarify anything by means of these concepts. And the minds of those who, by using them, believe to see things clearly, remain completely in the dark. Imagine what the terrible agonic dialectic of St. Paul would have done with these concepts!

Since individuality is that which is most universal, it is impossible to arrive at a mutual understanding on this basis. If the anarchists wish to survive, they must of necessity establish a State. And the communists must sustain themselves by leaning on the support of individual liberty.

Thus the most radical individualists must proceed to establish a community. The hermits join together to found a monastery, a cloister of monks (*monachos*), that is, of solitary recluses; of recluses who must aid one another. They must jointly bury their dead, and they must even make history since they do not create children.

It is thus the hermit only who approximates the ideal life of individualism. A Spanish man of science who, at almost sixty years of age, had set his mind on learning to ride a bicycle, told me that this was the most individualistic means of locomotion. I answered him: "No, Don José; the truly individualistic locomotion is to walk alone, on foot and barefooted, in places where there are no roads"; that is, to live alone, naked, in the desert.

Father Hyacinth (of whom we shall have to speak again), after his break with the Roman Catholic Church, wrote that the Anglo-Saxon race is "the race of the moral and strong family, the race of the energetic and free personality, the race of individual Christianity. . . ." And the opinion that Protestant Christianity and especially Calvinism is a manifestation of individualism, has been expressed quite often. But the truth is that individual Christianity is to be found nowhere except in the state of celibacy; Christianity in the hearth of the family is no longer pure Christianity but rather a compromise with the world. To follow Christ, it is necessary to leave father, mother, and brothers, wife and children. And if the continuation of the human race becomes thus impossible, so much the worse for the latter!

A universal monastery, however, that is, a monastery that would be open to all comers, is an impossibility. And for this reason there are two distinct classes of Christians: those of the world, of the *saeculum*—*saecula* means generations—the Christians in civil life, those who raise children destined for heaven; and then there are the pure Christians, the cloistered religious, the *monachos*. The former propagate the flesh and with it original sin, while the latter propagate the solitude of the spirit. It is possible, however, to carry the world into the midst of the cloister, to contaminate the *claustrum* with the *saeculum* and, conversely, to harbor the spirit of the cloister in the midst of the world.

Both categories of Christians, if they are dedicated to the religious life, live in inner contradiction and thus in agony. The religious who safeguards his virginity, the monk who preserves the seed of that flesh which he believes destined to rise again, who accepts the title of Father—or Mother, in the case of nuns—dreams of the immortality of the soul and of his survival in history.

St. Francis of Assisi anticipated that he would be remembered and spoken of, although St. Francis was not strictly speaking a religious recluse, a monk (*monachus*), but a brother (*fratello* = little brother), a friar. The civic Christian, on the other hand, the citizen and father of a family, lives, to be sure, in history, but he asks himself anxiously whether he may not thereby endanger his salvation. And if the man of the world who shuts himself up—or rather who is being shut up—in a monastery, is a tragic figure, the fate of the monk of the spirit, of the recluse who is forced to live in the world is even more tragic.

The state of virginity is for the Roman Catholic Apostolic Church more perfect in itself than that of marriage. It is true that the Church has raised the married state to the dignity of a sacrament, but it has done this as a concession to the world and to history. Meanwhile the instinct of paternity and maternity introduces anguish into the lives of those virginal men and women who have dedicated themselves to the Lord. In many convents of nuns a frenzied cult of the Child Jesus, the God-child, is being practiced.

Is it conceivable that Christendom—or perhaps

humanity—might at some future time be consti-
tuted in the manner of a bee-hive or an ant-hill,
with fathers and mothers on one side and sexless workers on the other? In the bee-hive and
the ant-hill the sexless bees and ants—why do we
use [in Spanish] the feminine gender and believe them to be females rather than abortive
males?—are the ones who work and who nurse
the sexually determined generations. They are
the maternal aunts or, if you will, the paternal
uncles. Ordinarily, it is the fathers and mothers
who work for the maintenance of their offspring,
while the proletarians work for the survival of
the flesh by producing those goods which perpetuate material life. But what about the spiritual
life? Among the Catholic peoples it is the monks
and nuns—the paternal uncles and the maternal
aunts—who maintain the Christian religious tradition, who educate the young. But since they
have to educate the young for the world, for the
saeculum, so as to prepare them for the task of
becoming fathers and mothers of families and
for the functions of civic and political life, the
inner contradiction in their teaching is obvious.
A bee can teach another bee how to construct a
cell, but it cannot teach a drone how to fertilize
the queen.

And this inner contradiction in the monastic
type of education that is handed out to future
citizens reaches its peak in that community which
is known as the "Society of Jesus." The Jesuits do

not like to be called monks or friars. A Benedictine or a Carthusian is a monk; a Franciscan or a Dominican is a friar. But after the Jesuits—in order to combat the Reformation with the secularization and generalization of primary education it inaugurated—had begun to dedicate themselves to the task of educating the laity, the citizens and future fathers of families, the other religious orders followed suit and became "jesuitized." In the end they came to regard public education as a commercial industry, the industsy of pedagogy. Instead of begging for alms, they became schoolmasters.

And thus Christianity, true Christianity, suffers agony at the hands of these masters of the *saeculum*. The pedagogy of the Jesuits is profoundly anti-Christian. The Jesuits hate mysticism. Their doctrine of passive obedience, of the three degrees of obedience as espoused in Iñigo of Loyola's famous letter to the Fathers and Brothers of Portugal, is an anti-Christian and at bottom anti-civic doctrine. This kind of obedience makes both civilization and progress impossible.

On February 24, 1911, Father Hyacinth wrote in his Journal: "Europe is condemned; and when we say Europe we mean Christianity. Europe need not fear to perish from the 'yellow peril' with which many people seek to scare it, even if this peril were doubled by the 'black peril': Europe carries within its bosom the two scourges which

by themselves suffice to kill it: Ultra-montanism *
and the Revolution. *Mane, Thekel, Phares.*** This
is why we must be content with *resisting* even
without the hope of victory, and we must keep
alive for an unknown future the double torch
of religion and of true civilization."

Napoleon said that a century hence Europe
would be either in the hands of the Cossacks or
in the hands of the Republicans, and he un-
doubtedly had in mind something quite similar to
what Father Hyacinth—who was a Napoleon of
sorts—meant when he was speaking of the Ultramontanists and the Revolutionaries, the only difference being that Napoleon was a child of Rousseau and Father Hyacinth a child of Chateaubriand: it ultimately amounts to the same thing.
What neither of them understood is that the
Cossacks turned into Republicans and the Republicans into Cossacks, that Ultramontanism became

* From the Latin *ultra montes* = on the other side
of the mountains (the Alps); a slogan used by liberal
and nationalist anticlericals to point to the supposed
dangers threatening from Roman Catholicism and the
Papacy.—*Translator.*

** These Aramaic words were (according to Daniel
5:1 sqq.) mysteriously written on the wall during
the banquet given by Belshazzar, the last king of
ancient Babylon. They mean: "counted" i.e., counted
are the days of the king's reign; "weighed" i.e.,
weighed were the king's works and found wanting;
"divided" i.e., divided will be Belshazzar's kingdom.
—*Translator.*

revolutionary and the Revolution became ultramontane. Neither the one nor the other foresaw the rise of Bolshevism and Fascism, nor did they foresee that entire monstrous and chaotic confusion which poor Oswald Spengler tried to explain in his musically construed "Decline of the West." This "decline" is of course nothing else but the agony of Christianity.

But what about the yellow peril? What about the black peril? The fact is that danger has no color. And what about the Moslem peril? To the extent that the Mohammedanism of the desert is forced to act upon the plane of history, it is bound to become civic and politically-minded; it is bound to become Christianized and eventually Christian; and war is—as Treitschke put it succinctly—politics *par excellence*. And thus historical Mohammedanism becomes agonic: it suffers in agony under the impact of proselytism.

I was speaking of progress; but progress is a civic, not a religious value.

What then about progress? Does history have a human or perhaps even a divine finality? Is history not rather fulfilled in every instant? For Christ and for those who believed with Him in the impending end of the world, the term progress was without meaning. There is no progress in sanctity: it is not possible to be more saintly today, in the twentieth century, than in the second or fourth or eleventh century. A Christian does not believe that progress aids in the salvation of the soul. Thus civic, historical progress is not indicative of the soul's ascending way to God. And herein lies another source of the agony of Christianity.

The doctrine of progress is the Nietzschean doctrine of the Superman. A Christian, on the other hand, believes that he must strive to become not a Superman but rather an Immortal Man, that is, a Christian.

Is there any progress after death? This is a question which the Christian who believes in the resurrection of the flesh and simultaneously in the immortality of the soul cannot avoid asking himself at one time or another. However, the majority of the simple evangelical believers like to picture for themselves the life to come as repose, as peace in the quietude of contemplation; or perhaps as the "eternalization of the instant," as a fusion of past and future, of memory and hope, as one everlasting present. The other life, the life of glory, is for the majority of simple believers a sort of monastic community of families, or rather a kind of phalanstery.*

It was Dante who was most daring in describing for us the communities on the other side of the tomb: those of Hell, Purgatory, and Paradise.

---

* A *phalanstery* (*phalansterium*) is the kind of economic and social community of families, fashioned after the monastic model, as proposed by the French "Utopian Socialist," Charles Fourier (1772-1837).— *Translator.*

But here both the condemned and the elect are alone and hardly ever grouped together socially. And if they do form a social group, Dante presents them to us not in his capacity as a Christian poet but as a Ghibelline politician. His *Divina Commedia* is a biblical rather than an evangelical comedy. And it is terrible in its agony.

Dante, the great despiser—the same Dante who felt pity for Francesca da Rimini—reserved his deepest contempt for that Pope who renounced the Papacy, for that poor Coelestine V, Pietro del Murrone, who was canonized by the Roman Church. He was the Pope who, according to Dante, "made the great renunciation because of his cowardice":

> *Che fece per viltate il gran rifiuto*
> (*Inferno*, III, 60).

And the poet places this Pope at the entrance of Hell between those who no longer hope for death, those who have lived without infamy and without praise; he places him among the poor tepid souls who have not fought, who have not known agony and whom one must pass by without even speaking of them:

> *Non raggioniam di lor, ma guarda e passa*
> (*Inferno*, III, 57).*

* "Let us not reason about them, but merely look at them and then pass on!"—*Translator*.

8

THE FAITH OF PASCAL

Applying what I have been saying about the agony of Christianity to a concrete case, I propose to speak about the agony of Christianity in the soul of Blaise Pascal. And I may be permitted to repeat here, with a few additional observations, what I wrote about the faith of Pascal in a special issue of the *Revue de Métaphysique et de la Morale* (April-June, 1923), on the occasion of the third centenary of Pascal's birth (June 19, 1623).

There I wrote the following lines: "The reading of the works bequeathed to us by Pascal, and particularly the reading of his *Pensées* (Thoughts), does not invite us to study a philosophy, but to learn to know a man, to penetrate into the sanctuary of the all-pervasive anguish of a soul, a totally naked, living soul, a soul wrapped in the haircloth of penance. And since the person who is undertaking this study is himself a human

being, he is running the risk referred to by Pascal
in the sixty-fourth *pensée:* 'I encounter all this
[of which I am here speaking] not in Montaigne
but in myself.' A risk? I really do not see any
risk. What constitutes the eternal strength of
Pascal is the fact that there are as many Pascals
as there are human beings who, while reading
him, recognize themselves in him and thus do
not confine themselves to merely understanding
him. It is in this manner that he is alive in those
who are in communion with his anguished faith.
I am therefore going to present my own Pascal.

"Since I am a Spaniard, my Pascal is Spanish
too, without any doubt. Was Pascal ever sub-
jected to Spanish influence? On two occasions, in
his *Pensées,* he quotes Santa Teresa (499, 868)
to tell us about that profound humility which
was the essence of her faith. He had studied two
Spaniards, one of whom he came to know by way
of Montaigne. Two Spaniards, or rather two Cata-
lans, Raimundus de Sabunde * and Martini, the
author of *Pugio fidei christianae* (The Dagger
of the Christian Faith). But I, who am a Basque
—and this means being Spanish in an even higher
degree—can discern the influence which two
Basque minds exerted on Pascal: the Abbé Saint-

---

* Raimundus de Sabunde (died 1437) was a scho-
lastic philosopher who tried to prove the truths of the
Christian faith from the study of nature. His main
work is the *Liber naturae,* later on named "Natural
Theology."—*Translator.*

Cyran,* the true founder of Port-Royal, and Iñigo of Loyola, the founder of the Society of Jesus. And it is interesting to see that the French Jansenism of Port-Royal and Jesuitism, which fought each other with such ferocity, owed their origin to two Basques. Perhaps this was more than a civil war: it was a war between brothers and almost between twin brothers, like the struggle between Jacob and Esau. And this same struggle was fought in the soul of Pascal.

"Pascal received the spirit of Loyola from the books of those Jesuits against whom he fought; but perhaps he discerned in these casuists the blockheads who were out to destroy the original intuition of Ignatius of Loyola.

"Among the letters of Iñigo of Loyola (St. Ignatius) there is one in particular which I was never able to forget in the course of my study of the soul of Pascal: it is the one he wrote in Rome, on March 26, 1553, and which he addressed to the Fathers and Brothers of the Society of Jesus in Portugal; it is the letter which lays down the three degrees of obedience. The first degree consists in the execution of that which is commanded, and this does not merit the name obedience, since it does not measure up to the excellence of this virtue; 'let us therefore ascend to the

* Jean Du Vergier de Hauranne (1581-1643), better known as the Abbot of Saint-Cyran, was one of the co-founders of Jansenism. He was imprisoned by Richelieu (1638-1643).—*Translator*.

second degree which consists in making one's own
the will of the Superior, in such a manner that
there is not only execution [of the command]
with respect to the effect, but a conformity in the
effect, in the form of an identity of wills in both
affirmation and negation. . . . But he who aspires
to that total and perfect oblation of the self which
transcends the will, must offer up his understanding (and this is a further and the highest degree
of obedience), and he must not only become *one
will* with his Superior but must become identical
with him in his feeling, and he must subject
his own judgment to his, inasmuch as a devout
will is capable of inclining the understanding.'
For 'every truly obedient person must strive to
unite his own feeling with that of his Superior.'
That is, he must accept as true whatever the Superior declares to be true. And to facilitate this
kind of obedience by rationalizing it with the
aid of a methodical scepticism (*scepsis* is a method
to rationalize that which is not evident),* the

---

* The meaning I give here to the word *scepsis*
(σκέψις) differs quite notably from what is commonly called *scepticism* (at least in Spain). *Scepsis*
denotes *search, research,* not *doubt,* unless by doubt
we mean the methodical doubt of Descartes. A sceptic
in this sense is opposed to the dogmatist, as a man
in search is opposed to the man who affirms prior to
any search. The sceptic studies in order to learn what
solution can be found, and maybe there is no solution. The dogmatist seeks nothing but proofs to sustain a dogma to which he adheres even prior to hav-

Jesuits invented that *probabilism* ** against which Pascal rebelled. He rebelled against it because he sensed its dangers within himself. Or is the famous argument of 'the wager' anything but a probabilist argument?

"The rebellious reason of Pascal was opposed to the third degree of obedience, but his feeling favored it. When, in 1705, the Bull *Vineam Domini Sabaoth* of Clement XI declared that in matters condemned by the Church respectful silence is not sufficient but that the heart must accept the decision in good faith, in the conviction that the decision is well founded *de iure* and *de facto*—would Pascal have bowed to this declaration if he had still been alive?

---

ing found any such proofs. The one loves the hunt, the other the spoils of the hunt. It is in this sense that the word *scepticism* must be understood as it is applied here to the Jesuits and to Pascal, and it is in the same sense that I am calling *probabilism* a "sceptical method."—*The author's footnote.*

** *Probabilism:* a system of moral theology that was first elaborated by the Dominican, Bartholemy Medina (1581). Its primary rule says: in the case of insoluble doubt concerning the moral legitimacy of an act, it is permissible to perform the act if sound reasons can be adduced in its favor, regardless of whether or not the opposite opinion can be sustained with equally valid reasons. In other words, the moral law is binding in conscience only when its obligatory nature can be recognized with indubitable certitude. Probabilism was defended by most Jesuit and many non-Jesuit moral theologians.—*Translator.*

"Pascal, who was inwardly so little submissive, who never succeeded in taming his reason, who was perhaps persuaded but hardly convinced of the truth of Catholic dogma, discussed with his own self the question of submission. He told himself that the person who does not submit himself in situations when it becomes necessary (*où il faut*), does not understand the force of reason (268). But what is the meaning here of the word *falloir* (to be necessary)? He told himself that to submit is to make use of one's reason and that in this precisely consists true Christianity (269); that reason would not submit itself if it were not able to judge that here are certain occasions where submission is necessary (270). But he also told himself that the Pope abhors and fears those savants who are not subservient to him by a special vow (873); and he rose in revolt against the threatening future dogma of papal infallibility (876) as representing the final step in the Jesuitic doctrine of the obedient submission of personal judgment, the basis of the Catholic faith.

"Pascal wished to submit himself; he preached to himself submission, while at the same time he was seeking *with sighs,* seeking without finding, and while the eternal silence of the infinite spaces frightened him. His was persuasion rather than conviction.

"His Faith? But in what did he believe? The answer depends on what one means by faith and by having faith. 'It is the heart which feels God, not reason; and this is faith: to feel God's presence in the heart, not in the reason" (278).

"In another place Pascal speaks of 'simple persons who believe without reasoning,' and he adds that 'God gives them love of Himself and hatred for themselves; He inclines their hearts to faith'; and again he says that 'no one would ever believe with a fruitbringing faith unless God had touched his heart' (284). A fruitbringing faith! Here we find ourselves again face to face with probabilism and the *wager*. Fruitbringing! Not without good reason does he write in another context: 'If only reason were truly reasonable. . . .' (73).

"Pascal, this poor mathematical 'thinking reed,' for whom Jesus shed 'these drops of blood, thinking of him in His agony (553, *Le Mystère de Jésus*)—this poor Blaise Pascal was seeking a fruitbringing faith which would deliver him from his reason. And he sought for it in submission and in spiritual habituation. 'This will make you believe, and it will dull your wits.'—'But this is precisely what I am afraid of.' 'Why? What have you got to lose?' (233). What have you got to lose? Here we have the utilitarian, probabilist, Jesuitic, irrational argument par excellence. This calculation of probabilities is nothing but a rationalization of chance, of irrationality.

"Did Pascal believe? He wanted to believe. And, according to William James, who was another probabilist, the 'will to believe' is the only kind of faith possible for a man endowed with a mathematical intellect, a lucid reason, and a sense of objectivity.

"Pascal turned against the rational Aristotelian proofs of the existence of God (242) and remarked that 'none of the canonical authors of Sacred Scripture had recourse to nature to prove the existence of God' (243); and as to the three media of faith—reason, custom, and inspiration—which he mentions (245), it suffices to read Pascal with an unbiased mind to feel that he did not believe in reason, nor could he ever, no matter how hard he tried, embrace his faith with his reason, that is, he became never convinced of what he had persuaded himself to believe. This then was his personal tragedy. And thus he sought his salvation in that scepticism which he loved, and in opposition to that inward dogmatism which was the cause of his suffering.

"In the first article which was dogmatically declared infallible in the canons of the Vatican Council [of 1870], an anathema was hurled against those who deny that the existence of God can be demonstrated rationally and scientifically, even though those who make the denial believe in Him (*"Naturali rationis humanae lumine certi cognoscere posse"*). Would not this anathema have struck out against Pascal? It may be said that Pascal, like so many others, did perhaps not believe that God ex-sists but rather that He in-sists, that Pascal searched for Him in the heart, that he did not need God for his experience of the vacant spaces nor for his scientific work, but did need Him in order not to feel himself annihilated by His absence.

"The inner life of Pascal strikes us as a tragedy. A tragedy that can be summarized in the words of the Gospel: 'I believe; Lord, help my unbelief!' (Mark 9:23). This obviously is not, properly speaking, belief but rather the will to believe.

"The truth of which Pascal speaks to us when he refers to the 'knowledge of the heart,' is not rational, objective truth; it is not reality, and he knew it well. All his effort was directed toward the creation of a supernatural world over and above the natural world. But was he convinced of the objective reality of this supernature? Persuaded, perhaps; convinced, no! And thus he sermonized to himself.

"And what difference is there between this position and that of the Pyrrhonists,* those Pyrrhonists against whom Pascal fought so valiantly because he felt that inwardly he was a Pyrrhonist himself? Yes, there is one difference: Pascal did not resign himself, did not succumb to doubt, to

---

* *Pyrrhonists:* so named after Pyrrhon, a Greek philosopher (ca. 360-270 B.C.), the founder of scepticism. The Pyrrhonists of the seventeenth century taught that identically valid reasons can be advanced in favor or against a proposition. One must therefore refrain from judgment and strive for perfect equanimity (*ataraxía*). *Translator.*

negation, to *scepsis;* he needed the dogma and he searched for it, deliberately dulling his reason. His logic was not dialectical but rather polemical. He was not looking for a synthesis beyond thesis and antithesis but, like Proudhon, another Pascalian thinker, he continued living in the midst of the contradiction. 'We cherish struggle above everything; we like it better than victory' (135). He actually was afraid of victory because he feared that his reason might be victorious over his faith. 'The most cruel war into which God can plunge a man in this life is to deprive him of that conflict which He has come to bring into this world' (498). Pascal was afraid of peace, and he had a valid motive: he was afraid of the encounter with nature, which is reason.

"But in a human being, a true and complete human being, in a rational being conscious of his reason, can there exist a faith which recognizes the possibility of a rational demonstration of the existence of God? Can there exist the possibility of that third degree of obedience, in accordance with the precept of Iñigo of Loyola? One can reply: certainly not without grace. And what is grace? Another tragic evasion.

"When Pascal went down on his knees to implore the Supreme Being (233), he asked that his reason be granted the gift of submission. Did he receive the gift? He wanted to submit, but he found repose only in and with death. And today he lives on in those who, like we ourselves, have touched his naked soul with the nakedness of their own souls."

To these lines I can only add that Pascal, in his association with the recluses of Port-Royal—and a recluse himself—was not a monk; he had not taken a vow of celibacy or virginity, although he may well have died in the state of virginity (we don't know); but he was a man of civic life, a citizen, and even a politician. His campaign against the Jesuits was at bottom a political and civic campaign, and his "Provincial Letters" are a political manifesto. Here we are face to face with another inner contradiction in the life of Pascal and can discern another source of the agony which Christianity underwent in his soul.

The same man who wrote the *Pensées* wrote the *Lettres Provinciales*, and both works sprang from the same source.

Let us first take note that they are *Pensées* (Thoughts), not *Ideas*. An idea is something hard and fixed; a thought is something fluid, changeable and free. A thought begets another thought; an idea tends to choke another idea. One might say that a thought is an idea in action, or that it is a principle of action within an idea; an idea is a dogma. Idea-men are prisoners of their ideas; they rarely think. The "Thoughts" of Pascal are a polemic and agonic piece of writing. If he had ever completed the apologetic work which he intended to write, we should have in our hands something quite different and vastly inferior to the "Thoughts." This latter work could never arrive at a conclusion: an agonic work is not a work of apologetics.

I have just been reading the following passage in Leo Chestov's *La nuit de Gethsémani, essai sur la philosophie de Pascal* (*Les Cahiers Verts, publiés sous la direction de Daniel Halévy;* Paris: Barnard Grasset, 1923): ". . . An *apologia* must defend God in the face of man; it must then of necessity and *nolens volens* acknowledge human reason as ultimate arbiter. If it had been granted to Pascal to terminate his labors, he could have done nothing else but give expression to that which is acceptable to human beings and their reason." Maybe; but human beings seem to accept *nolens volens* Pascal's *déraisonnements* (irrational arguments).

We believe that Chestov is mistaken when he says that history is inexorable for apostates—Pascal was an apostate of reason—and that one cannot really hear the voice of Pascal despite the candles that are being burned before his image. One can hear the voice of Pascal very well, and one can hear him speak in agony. Chestov was able to hear this voice, and this is why he could write his beautiful essay.

"It is not Pascal," Chestov adds, "but rather Descartes who is regarded as the father of modern philosophy; and it is not from Pascal but from Descartes that we are willing to accept the truth; for where should we seek the truth if not in philosophy? Such is the judgment of history: one admires Pascal and one bypasses him. And against this judgment there is no appeal."

Is this really so? One does not just pass by after having once admired, after having loved someone. Dante's *guarda e passa* one reserves for those whom one despises, not for those whom one admires, whom one loves. And is it correct to say that truth is sought only in philosophy?

What is genuine philosophy? Perhaps only that which is called metaphysics. But there is also the meta-erotic, which is beyond love, and the meta-agonic, which is beyond agony and beyond dream.

The *Lettres Provinciales* grew out of the same spirit as the *Pensées* and express another agonic experience; they are another treatise filled with contradictions. The Christian who in these letters turns against the Jesuits is well aware of their human, all-too-human side, of the civic and social aspects of their order. He knows that without the compromises of their lax morality, moral life in the world would be impossible; that the Jesuit doctrine of grace (or rather of free will) is the only one that makes allowances for a normal civic life. But at the same time he feels that this doctrine is anti-Christian. The Augustinian as well as the Calvinistic and Jansenistic ethics contribute no less than the moral philosophy of the Jesuits to the agony of Christianity.

It cannot be denied that ethics and religion are two diffierent things. Already in the domain of ethics as such—or rather, in the sphere of morality, for the term ethics smacks a little of pedantry —being good and doing the good are not the same. There are certain people who die without having transgressed the law and without having desired the good. And, conversely, the thief who died on a cross at the side of Christ accused that other outlaw—who asked the Master to save them both if He was really the Christ—of blasphemy, asking: "Have you no fear of God, when you are undergoing the same sentence? We two are justly being punished, for we receive the due reward for our deeds; but this man has committed no crime." And, turning to Jesus, he said: "Lord, remember me when you come into your kingdom." And Christ answered him: "Truly, I promise you that this day you shall be with Me in Paradise" (Luke 23:39-44). The thief who repented in the hour of death believed in the kingdom of Christ, the kingdom of God, which is not of this world; he believed in the resurrection of the flesh, and Christ promised him Paradise, that biblical garden in which our first parents fell from grace. And a Christian must believe that every Christian and even that every man will repent in the

hour of death; that death in itself is already a
kind of repentance and expiation; that death puri-
fies the sinner. Juan Sala y Serrallonga, the ban-
dit of whom the eminent Catalan poet Juan Mara-
gall sang, said to the hangman in the hour of his
death on the gallows—to atone for all his sins,
anger, envy, gluttony, lust, avarice, robbery, murder: "I shall die reciting the *Credo*, but do not
hang me by the neck before I have said: I believe
in the resurrection of the flesh!"

Did Pascal in the "Provincial Letters" defend
the moral values, or rather the values of the police force, against the strictly religious, comfort-
ing values upheld by the Jesuits? Or did the
Jesuits represent an accommodating police force
with a casuistic morality standing arrayed against
the purity of religion? Both theses can be sustained with equal facility. The fact is that there
exist two different kinds of religion. This "du-
plicity" or ambivalence is the essential precondi-
tion of the agony of Christianity and of the agony
of our civilization. And if the *Pensées* and the
Lettres Provinciales seem to be mutually contradictory, the reason is that each of these works
is contradictory in itself.

"One might say," writes Chestov, "that Pascal
would have remained the Pascal of the *Lettres
Provinciales* if he had not encountered the 'abyss.'"
But he did encounter the abyss while he was
writing the *Lettres Provinciales* or, rather, the

Lettres Provinciales rose from the same abyss as the *Pensées*. In his search for greater depth in morality, Pascal arrived at religion; in testing Roman Catholicism and Jansenism he arrived at Christianity; for Christianity lies hidden in the ground of Catholicism, and religion lies hidden in the depth of morality.

Pascal, the man of contradiction and of agony, foresaw that Jesuitism, with its doctrine of passive intellectual obedience and implicit faith, kills struggle and agony and therewith the very life of Christianity. And, nonetheless, it was Pascal who in a moment of agonic despair had written the phrase, *"cela vous abêtira"* (this will dull your reason). And it is a fact that a Christian can "dull his reason," that is, commit intellectual suicide. What a Christian cannot do is *abêtir* another person, kill the intellect of another person. But this is precisely what the Jesuits are doing; only, in trying to dull the reason in others, they have dulled their own. In treating all men like children, they have themselves become infantile in the saddest sense of the term. Today there is hardly anything more puerile than a Jesuit—I mean particularly a Spanish Jesuit. All their supposed cunning is purely legendary. Anyone can outwit them, although they believe themselves to be the most keen-witted. History, historical evolution, vital and concrete daily history, is for them a sort of magical comedy. They fall into all kinds of traps. Leo Taxil * completely deceived them! In Jesuitism, Christianity has lost its agony; it no longer struggles, it no longer is alive but dead and buried. The cult of the Sacred Heart of Jesus, this "Hierocardiocracy," is the tomb of the Christian religion.

"Do not ask me this question, for I am ignorant; Holy Mother Church has learned men who know the answer." In this manner the catechism composed by the Jesuit Father Astete—the most widely used catechism in Spain—answers a certain question. And these "learned men," by their failure to teach certain things to those who have implicit faith, have in the end themselves forgotten the answers and have become as ignorant as their pupils.

Alain ** writes in his *Propos sur le christianisme* (44, Pascal): "Pascal is constantly and essentially in opposition—an orthodox heretic." An orthodox heretic! Exactly! "Heterodox orthodoxy" would be a moribund contradiction in which the antithetical terms destroy each other; for "an-

* Leo Taxil (Gabriel Jogand, 1854-1907) was a French anticlerical and the author of pornographic books. After his "conversion" to Roman Catholicism he began to hurl sensational accusations against the Freemasons, based on fraudulent documents. He finally admitted his many deceptions.—*Translator*.

** Alain (Emile Auguste Chartier, 1868-1951): a French writer with a strong anticlerical bias.— *Translator*.

other" doctrine—*heteros*—may be true—*orthos*—, since that which differs from something else is *one*, and therefore "heretic" is a much clearer term. For a heretic (*haereticus*) is a person who freely chooses a doctrine, who freely holds an opinion—freely?—and who can freely judge which is the right doctrine, who can create a doctrine and freely recreate a dogma which the others profess to believe. Did not something of this sort happen to Pascal in the course of his research in geometry? St. Paul says in a certain passage— I do not have at hand the exact reference, and the peculiar rhythm of my life does not permit me to locate it at the moment—that with respect to a certain doctrine he is a heretic. "In this matter I am a heretic," he says at the end of his epistle (and I shall not attempt here to translate his Greek—something which is so frequently done with evangelical and other texts); but what he really meant to say was: "In regard to this matter I profess a particular personal opinion rather than the current one." He wanted to say that in this particular point he is setting himself apart from the commonly accepted sense and is clinging to the more authentic and personal meaning, on the basis of a free examination. And who would dare say that the authentic personal sense is not occasionally capable of discovering certain principles of the common sense, that heresy does not sometimes create orthodoxy? All orthodoxies were heresies in the beginning, and to rethink, to re-create the commonplaces, to transform ideas into thoughts, is the best means to free oneself of their falsehoods. And by rethinking the ideas of Catholicism—the ideas which the others professed to believe—Pascal, the heretic, transformed these *ideas* into *thoughts,* transformed the Catholic dogma into living truth and thus recreated ortho-doxy. All this, however, was of course the very opposite of implicit faith (*Köhlerglaube*), of the blind and infantile faith of the Jesuits.

The man who wants to "bestialize" (*abêtir*) his reason—by offering it up as a sacrifice, alone and freely—vanquishes the beast within himself and rises above the bestial much more than the man who obeys a Superior *per inde ac cadaver* (ca-daver-like) in accordance with the stipulation of the third degree of submission, that is, by the surrender of his intelligence. The latter believes that what the Superior regards as better is *ipso facto* better; he may even pray to a stick planted in the monastery garden, simply because the Prior has commanded him to do so. This is of course nothing but a sportive exercise and a comedy on the part of the one who commands as well as on the part of the one who obeys, since neither of them believes that the stick will take roots, grow leaves and flowers and bear fruit like the staff of St. Joseph, the Patriarch; and so all this is of no more value than any conventional game.

It is nothing but a conventional game played in order to tame human pride, and the question is never asked whether there is not a greater pride hidden in this kind of obedience. For if it is written that he who humbles himself will be exalted, this surely does not mean that he who has humbled himself in the face of another's self-exaltation will be exalted. This kind of obedience has bred the inflated collective pride—the Luciferian pride—of the Society of Jesus.

Pascal was scandalized by the small talk of the Jesuits, by their fine "distinctions" and their punctilious pedantry. And these things are no trifles! The *scientia media*,* the theory of *probabilism*, etc., etc. But they must of course make a play with liberty, and so they say: *In necessariis unitas, in dubiis libertas, in omnia caritas* (in things necessary, unity; in doubtful propositions, liberty; in all things, charity). And in order to be able to play the game of liberty, they enlarge the field of doubt and create doubt where there is no reason for doubting. One must only read, for exam-

---

* A central concept of the Spanish Jesuit Luis de Molina's (1553-1600) doctrine on predestination, grace, and free will is that of the *scientia media*, that is, the divine foreknowledge which God has of free human acts within a set of predetermined conditions and circumstances. According to "Molinism," man needs for his natural acts no more than the simultaneous divine cooperation (*concursus divinus*) without any positive divine predetermination (*praedeterminatio physica*).—*Translator.*

ple, the Metaphysics of P. Suarez * to see a man amusing himself with splitting a hair into four parts longitudinally and thereupon tying the four strands into a braid. Or when they engage in historical studies—what they call history goes rarely much beyond the realm of archaeology—they amuse themselves with counting the hairs of the tresses of the Sphinx, chiefly because by doing this they can evade the glance of her eyes. What amount of labor goes into the chore of dulling one's own reason and that of others!

When someone tells you of a Jesuit—I repeat again: in particular a Spanish Jesuit—who is supposed to have studied and learned a great deal, don't believe it. This is much like someone telling you that one of them has travelled a great deal when in reality he has covered twenty miles daily walking back and forth in the little garden of his place of residence.

No wonder that Blaise Pascal, this genuine recluse, could not come to terms with these militant soldiers!

And then there is science! In one of the Society's Spanish Novitiates—the one at Oña—a friend of mine who in his capacity as a physi-

---

* Francisco Suarez (1548-1617) was a Spanish Jesuit theologian and philosopher and the most influential of post-medieval scholastics; he was instrumental in developing the modern Roman Catholic doctrine of natural law, political theory, and international law.—*Translator*.

cian paid a visit to one of the novices, saw in the gallery of the cloistered section of the house a painting representing the Archangel Michael with Satan crouching at his feet. And Satan, the rebellious angel, held in his hand—a microscope! A microscope—the symbol of hyper-analysis.

These gentlemen, then, are trying to arrest and evade the agony of Christianity; and they accomplish this by assassinating it. To deliver Christianity from its agony they administer the fatal opiate of their spiritual exercises and their education. In the end they will have made of the Roman Catholic religion something resembling Tibetan Buddhism.

9

FATHER HYACINTH

While I was working on this anguished essay, I came upon the three volumes by Albert Houtin which deal with the anguished and tortured life of Father Hyacinth Loyson. The individual volumes bear the following titles: "Father Hyacinth in the Roman Church (1827-1869)"; "Father Hyacinth, Catholic Reformer (1869-1893)"; and "Father Hyacinth, the Lonely Priest (1893-1912)" [Paris: Librarie Emile Nourry]. I read or rather devoured these books with growing anguish. Here is one of the greatest tragedies I have ever encountered, comparable to and even more intense than the tragedy of Pascal, Lamennais, and Amiel. For in the case of Loyson it is the tragedy of a "Father," a priest, although according to the revelations contained in the new edition of Amiel's *Journal intime*—after it was rescued from the possession of the Calvinist hypocrite who was its first editor—there is manifest in the tragedy of

Amiel the agony of his virginity, which provides the clue of the mystery of his anguished life as a poor professor of aesthetics in Calvin's and Jean-Jacques' Geneva.

Father Hyacinth! Father! It is precisely in his paternity that the ground and the essence of his tragedy, of the agony of *his* Chrisianity, can be found. He left the Church to get married; he married to be able to have children, to perpetuate himself in the flesh, to ensure the resurrection of the flesh. But let us take a look at the history of his life.

Father Hyacinth, who is now almost a forgotten man, whom one is ready to entomb in history, in the soul's immortality, entertained in his lifetime close relations with many of the most prominent men of his epoch, such as Montalembert, Le Play, Victor Cousin, Father Gratry, Renan, Guizot, Msgr. Isoard, Doellinger, Dupanloup, Pusey, Cardinal Newman, Strossmayer, Taine, Gladstone, Jules Ferry, etc., etc. He did earn the insults of that mad dog, Louis Veuillot.

As he said himself, the ground of his soul was "an inextricable mixture of mysticsm and rationalism" (I, 7). He did not leave behind a single work which can be read in print, except his life as written down by Houtin (I, 10) under Loyson's personal direction. "Lamartine's early *Méditations poétiques* awakened his thought, his feeling, his life, and he developed into manhood in loneliness, at the foot of the Pyrenees, under the stim-

ulating influence of nature, poetry, and religion
(I, 26). Not under the influence of the Gospel. But
he owed his intellectual formation more to Chateaubriand, that great sophist, that great falsifier
of the genius of Christianity, than to Lamartine
(I, 27). He grew up under the influence of that
Chateaubriand who wrote about the loves of Atala
and René. In the Seminary of Saint-Sulpice he
received the "revelation" of the Virgin (I, 52),
the Virgin-Mother. And concomitantly with this
revelation—the revelation of paternity—came the
preoccupation with civic life, with history, with
politics, with the world which endures, with
fame, with the immortality of the soul. "I am
passing through this life," he told himself, "without love and without exerting influence. When my
bones will lie blanched in the earth, when they
will have lost their shape and when their dust
will no longer bear a name among men, what
of myself will remain in this world?" (I, 69). He
desired to remain in this world because he was
of this world and not of the kingdom of God.

He entered Saint-Sulpice, he passed through the
Dominican Order like a fugitive shadow, and not
long thereafter he became a member of the
Discalced Carmelites; it was then that the great
tragedy began. He started his fight against the
egotism of the body, which is as odious as the
egotism of the individual (I, 110).

And then commenced the temptations of the
flesh. "The loyal and enthusiastic practice of

celibacy had led me into a false and unhealthy condition. . . . I am in love not with one particular woman, but with woman" (I, 115). But what he really stood in need of was a child of the flesh in whom he could survive. In the small Carmelite monastery of Passy, at the age of thirty-seven, he dreamed "of birds' songs and also of the songs and games of children" (I, 222). When he converted Mme. Meriman, who was to become his wife, it was he who was totally converted by her, converted to paternity, to the kingdom of this world. There grew up among these two people a deceptive mystical union, not the kind of friendship that existed between St. Francis of Assissi and St. Clare, not the kind which existed between St. Francis of Sales and Joan of Chantal, nor the kind which existed between Santa Teresa of Jesus and St. John of the Cross. Nor did sexuality play a part in the love of Father Hyacinth. He was simply possessed by the idea of paternity, by the frantic desire to ensure the resurrection of the flesh.

So let us put aside for the moment the rest of his agonies and let us concentrate on this particular agony. First of all, he celebrated his mystical betrothal to Mme. Meriman. He was at that time forty-five years of age. Shortly thereafter he married her. At the age of forty he knew no more about women than what he had been taught in the confessional (II, 9); he did not "know" them, as David did not "know" Abisag. And much later,

as an old man, at the age of eighty-two, he wrote
that one is not "a priest in the full sense save in
marriage" (II, 122). A priest? What he really
wanted to say was: a father! And he cried out:
"God and Woman!" (II, 123). What he meant
was: God and the resurrection of the flesh! That
"force superior to my will" which "with astound-
ing and at times frightening persistence" (II, 81)
pushed him into marriage, was the force of un-
satisfied paternity. This was the nature of his love.
"The intent to destroy it would be tantamount to
suicide" (II, 82): it would mean perennial self-
destruction! When, at the age of eighty, he wrote:
"The great vision of God and of the Eternal City,
which is always present in my consciousness and
even more in my subconsciousness, has been *my
joy* and my strength" (II, 350-351), he was not
aware of the fact that this subconsciousness was
the genius of the species of which Schopenhauer,
the pessimistic bachelor, spoke: the genius of
the species in search of a faith in the resurrection of the flesh. What Loyson needed was a son.
He could not allow the dead to bury their dead
and permit those who believed themselves alive
to engender other living creatures, and take himself refuge in the community of those who believe that the end of the world is at hand. "May
the Church and the child be born jointly, for the
greater glory and the kingship of our God!" (II,
142). He had to make sure of the perpetuity of
the flesh in order to ensure the perpetuity of the

spirit; he wanted to give to his son physical life in order to transmit to him and infuse into him a soul (II, 147). He wanted to make of his child a monk, a replica of himself: he wanted to transmit the monastic vocation by means of the blood: "If God should give me a son, I will tell him while pouring the baptismal water upon his forehead: remember some day that you are of the race of the monks of the West! Be a monk, that is, a recluse in the midst of this age of incredulity and fanaticism, of superstition and immorality; be a monk, that is, be consecrated to the God of your father, to adore Him like John the Baptist, in the desert of the soul, to announce His coming" (II, 151). He wanted to transmit his loneliness and his agony! To our knowledge, St. John the Baptist was not a father: he was much too firmly convinced of the impending end of the world!

And so Loyson wanted his son to become a monk, to inherit his father's Christian solitude. But a hereditary monachism is bound to become political, and Father Hyacinth abhorred politics, which pertains to the realm of this world. And yet he had to become entangled in politics, since he was a fleshly father, and carnal paternity pertains to the kingdom of this world, not to the kingdom of God, and it is immersed in history. The nepotism of the Popes and bishops and parsons who are out to protect the worldly careers of their nephews, is a thing of this world, not of the Christian's world. And many of the supposedly

religious vocations of the parsons—not the vocations of monks and friars—are actually family affairs and have to do with economic considera-
tions. "The business of the parson endures forever," as the saying goes. Politics and still more
politics!

Yet, on the other hand, heritage is the firmest
basis of any definitive political activity. It is inherited qualities that have given strength to that
British political aristocracy whose members are
educated according to political tradition. The
young British Lord listens to political talk in his
home from the days of his childhood. There exist
in England entire dynasties of conservative political traditionalists. On the one hand, they want to
perpetuate their race; on the other hand, they
understand that politics is an affair of the world
of the flesh, the world of inheritance, the world
in which the dead bury their dead—the world
of history.

We are sometimes told that Christ did not institute the Church, that the Church is of necessity a thing of this world, and that what Christ did
institute was the Eucharist. But the Eucharist,
the sacrament of bread and wine, the bread that
is eaten and the wine that is drunk, is likewise
a thing of this world, since the bread is changed
into flesh and the wine into blood. All this is indicative of the struggle against death, which is
agony.

Father Hyacinth needed a son not only of his

love but also of his faith (II, 199), a son who
would give him faith in the resurrection of the
flesh. And perhaps he asked the Mother of the
Creator for such a son, repeating the words of
Psalm 21: "My soul shall live for him, and my
race shall serve him" (II, 161). One must read the
pages of burning faith, with their undertone of
despair, which Loyson wrote when his son Paul
was born to him. He wanted to turn his home into
a monastery (II, 170). And at the same time he
was tortured by the thought of the immortality
of the soul and of a life in history. "There will be
others in whom I shall live on, children of my
blood and children of my word" (II, 269). In his
"Testament" he bequeathed his faith and his hope
—what he wanted to believe and to hope—"to
my son who will, I hope, be more the son of my
soul than the son of my blood" (II, 299), to the
son whom he called "flesh of my flesh, breath of
my soul, and fruit of my life" (II, 303), the son
whose death he had to witness. "My beloved son
will perhaps follow me soon into the unfathom-
able mystery of death; he may even precede me,"
he wrote at the age of seventy-nine (II, 393),
and the son indeed preceded him into the mystery, but he left behind some grandchildren. And
Father Hyacinth, one of the most distinguished
representatives of the "stupid nineteenth century"
did in no way exploit the death of this son in
whom he loved himself with a frenzied love. Nor
did he, in all truthfulness, envy his own father,

although the latter—despite the fact that he was
a man of distinction and even a poet—had not
bequeathed to his son a name in history. If he
was envious of anything, it was paternity as such.

Compared with this agony, the agony of ideas
counted very little. When he was still in the
Carmelite monastery, Father Hyacinth wrote: "By
the grace of God, I want to come to live in such
a way as if I had to die in the following instant.
. . . The Church is present here too, in this very
garden, in this very cell" (II, 118); but he was
unable to evoke and retain this sentiment. He
spoke of "the more scientific and more universal
needs of his interior life" (I, 144). Scientific needs!
How far have the masses progressed in assimilat-
ing the temptations of science to the temptations
of the flesh! Why was Father Hyacinth scandalized by that profoundly Christian sentiment enun-
ciated by Msgr. Darboy: "Your error lies in the
assumption that man has something to accomplish
in this life. It is a counsel of prudence to do
nothing and to persevere." * To this the poor
Father added in his diary: "This scepticism filled
my soul with bitterness and doubts" (I, 308).

* Georges Darboy (1813-1871) was the Archbishop
of Paris. At the Vatican Council (1870) he was one
of those prelates who were opposed to the declaration
of the dogma of Papal Infallibility, but he submitted
after the promulgation of the dogma. He was shot as
one of sixty-three hostages during the uprising of the
French "Commune" in 1871.—*Translator.*

Scepticism? It was rather the Christian wisdom contained in these words which filled him with doubts.

This poor Father, who carried two different kinds of men within himself, asked himself the question: "Is there no third man who could reconcile the two? Or will the third man arise only in eternity?" (I, 280). And thus these two were fighting a war within him: on the one side stood the father and the civic man hungering for the resurrection of the flesh and for the immortality of the soul, and on the other side the Christian, the recluse, the monk.

Father Hyacinth left the Church when the dogma of the infallibility of the Pope was promulgated; he left the Church to get married and to have children. He buried Lamartine, another dead man, on March 3, 1869; he had an interview with Pius IX; he mingled with Protestants, Saint-Simonists, Jews, and rationalists in the *International and Permanent League for Peace;* he joined the so-called Old Catholics; he founded the National Catholic Church of Geneva and served as its pastor; later on, he became a member of the Anglo-Catholic Church of Paris; he travelled in the United States, lecturing on religion; already far advanced in age, he wanted to become a Roman Catholic priest of the Oriental Rite, where priests are permitted to marry; he dreamed of a union of Christians, Jews, and Moslems, and he reached the peak of his life's prolonged agony at the age of eighty-five, as a widower and an orphan of his son. Yes, an orphan!

Moreover, he had to fight, to be in agony, to provide bread for his wife and his children, bread for his own flesh. Some impresario in the United States proposed to take him on a lecture tour— whether with or without fanfare we do not know— and if this plan had materialized, the young girls would without doubt have asked his auto- graph for their albums or postal cards. For Father Hyacinth was a sensation! If there had existed newspapers in Judaea at the time of Christ, how much more terrible would have been His agony!

Father Hyacinth fought against Ultramonta- nists and rationalists, but he fought above all against himself. Prior to his marriage he wrote to the woman who was to become the mother of his son and his own mother: "I bear the doubt in my innermost spirit; I have carried it within me ever since I began to think; but I carry faith in the ground of my soul" (II, 17). What kind of distinction did he make between "spirit" and "soul"? Moreover, to think is to doubt; to have ideas is something else again. Deism serves life, not death. And the Christian lives in order to die. "All these men," he wrote in his eighty-sixth year, "have done exactly nothing, since, while they were speaking in the name of God, *they had not seen Him*. And I, who have seen Him, have not done anything either" (II, 97-98). The Scrip- tures tell us that he who sees the face of God

must die. But so must the one who does not see
His face!

Father Hyacinth abhorred politics, and yet he
had to become involved in politics. While he desired to rekindle the agony of David, he was in
the service of Solomon. The masses which he
celebrated after he had left the Roman Church,
were essentially political masses. And in the final
period of his life as a Carmelite "he no longer
celebrates mass every day, and when he does say
mass he enjoys the liberty of a Protestant who
believes in the Real Presence [of Christ in the
Eucharist], without having scruples about trans-
substantiation" (I, 294). This means nothing at
all unless it means that the good Father did not
celebrate mass, did not consecrate the species
[of bread and wine], did not pronounce the words
prescribed by the ritual, the words upon which,
according to Roman Catholic doctrine, depends
the mystery, the miracle, regardless of the state
of the celebrant's soul, since the sacrament works
ex opero operato and not *ex opere operantis*.*

* The Latin terms may be roughly translated by
"objectively" and "subjectively." In other words, according to Roman Catholic doctrine, the sacramental
grace is "objective" or "real" in the sense that its
efficacy is thwarted only if the recipient of the sacrament intentionally posits an obstacle. In the case of
the sacrament of the Eucharist, the efficacy does not
depend on the state of the soul of the officiating
priest.—*Translator*.

To put it differently: to avoid committing a sacrilege, he may have committed a fraud by making of the mass a fanciful comedy.

Father Hyacinth fought against Ultramontanists and against unbelieving rationalists, and he went so far as to say that Christianity is a "middle term" (II, 218). All this goes to show that Christianity was in agony within his own self.

He fought against fanatical Pharisees who asked him whether or not it was legitimate to pay tribute to the Empire and to rebel against the Roman Pontiff, to marry in order to beget children of the flesh; and he fought against Sadducean sceptics who asked him whose wife—among the seven brothers who had possessed her—the woman would be on the day of their resurrection from the dead.

He praised the Mormons, who believe in the resurrection of the flesh. And here we have one of the most striking characteristics of his agony: "(1) They have understood," he wrote, "that in the last analysis this is a question of religious economy; that Protestantism is just as much off the track as Romanism; and that the kingdom of God is to come upon this earth—but not a kingdom in which one will live like the angels of heaven, without getting married and without begetting children. (2) They have understood that theocracy is the true government of human societies" —not of divine societies—; that "if Rome has misused the idea of theocracy, this is no argument against the principle as such. (3) They have understood that sex relations are part of religion. They have been in error with respect to polygamy, but we ourselves are in error more seriously. The hypocritical kind of polygamy which has entered the social life of modern Christianity is much more unhealthy and more worthy of condemnation than the kind of religiously consecrated polygamy practised by the Mormons with—as I do not hesitate to add—its definite moral safeguards for wives and children. (4) I also praise the Mormons because of their reverence for the Old Testament. Christian heathenism has become too much estranged from its Israelite cradle. We no longer feel ourselves the sons and heirs of the Patriarchs and the Prophets; we have broken all ties with the Kingdom of David. . . ." And with the kingdom of Solomon? "We no longer have anything but disdain for the Priesthood of Aaron" (II, 249).

This poor Father who experienced the agony of Christianity in his soul, wished to return to the days when Jesus, the Christ, the Son Who was no father, fought against ultramontane Pharisees and Sadducean rationalists. The above quoted passage on the Mormons is dated February 28, 1884; on March 16 of the same year, while he was still travelling in the United States, he wrote: "But now I must return to my French blind alley to be crushed anew between the Ultramontanists and the sceptics, between the revolutionaries and the reactionaries. *Deduc me, Domine, in via tua et ingrediar in veritatem tuam!*" (II, 250) [Guide me, Lord in Thy ways, and I shall enter into Thy Truth].

In one particular passage Father Hyacinth stated that "Christianity has perhaps been surpassed" (II, 254), and this he said while he was in the midst of anguished reflections. "I am unable to create the world that lives in my thoughts or, rather, I can create it only in my thoughts which pass away, not in my deeds which endure" (II, 269). He was unable to believe in the eternity of the Word by Which everything was created; he wanted to believe in the eternity of the Fact, of the Flesh, and maybe of the Letter.

His last years, after his retirement from active life, from 1893 to 1912, from his sixty-sixth to his eighty-fifth year, were the most tragic years of his life, the years of his greatest solitude. He lived to a robust "Davidic" old age. He lived through years upon years of agony. "I suffer much. I live to witness a dolorous and *dishonorable* agony" (III, 113). Always this reminder of the things of this world! What caused his greatest suffering was his religious isolation. Like Jacob, he was fighting alone with the angel of the Lord, from sunset to dawn, crying: "Tell me your name!" (Genesis 32:24-29). He felt there were alive within himself two personalities, both equally sincere and equally religious-minded— Loyson the Christian and Loyson the monotheist (III, 134), and the fact that he felt this discordance between Christianity and monotheism is proof of the moral and religious depth of his soul's agony. His son Paul, the son of his flesh, came to the aid of the monotheist against the Christian. Paul was one of the dead who wanted to bury his deceased father. The simple fact is that one cannot without agony be simultaneously a father and a Christian. Christianity is the religion of the Son, the Virgin-Son, not the religion of the Father. Humanity began with Adam, to terminate in Christ. "For the greatest sin of man is ever to have been born," as our Spanish poet Calderon de la Barca says. This is the true original sin.

Father Hyacinth wrote to his son: "As you have said, we must leave every soul face to face with the Eternal, and no one save God has the right to judge" (III, 140). "He believed that his place was no longer at the side of his contemporaries, but in solitude, waiting for death or perhaps for that which is on the other side of death" (III, 143). What kind of solitude was this? He remembered the words which his son had spoken to him: "My poor father, at the end of your life you have no church left except that of your family" (III, 147). And he wrote: "I remain alone

with Emily . . . and with God" (III, 148). Alone
with the spirit and with the flesh; with the immortality of the soul and with the resurrection
of the flesh. M. Seillière, commenting on a judgment which Emile Ollivier passed on Father
Hyacinth, said of him that he was "a Rousseauvian rather than a rational Catholic" (III, 418).
Aside from the absurdity of speaking of a "rational Christian," this statement would be in
order if Father Hyacinth were one of the heirs
of Rousseau. But he actually descended from
Chateaubriand, or perhaps from Rousseau by way
of Chateaubriand. For is not *René*, after all, a
"Rousseauvian Catholic?"

Father Hyacinth wanted to revert to the "Aryan
ways of life which preceded Christianity" (III,
176). When his wife—his mother—died, he was
eighty-three years old and still a child. It was at
that time that he wrote the lines, "There is a
law, superior to the world and to God, which
prevents the dead from speaking to the living and
to manifest themselves in any fashion. The at-
tempts of the spiritists and the experiences of the
mystics protest in vain against that sacred law.
Oh, silence of the dead! Oh, silence of God!"
(III, 185). Pascal, who was not a father, had
anticipated and never transcended this emphatic
assertion. "If the darkness and silence in Sheol
[Hades, the tomb] should have lasted to this day,
it would certainly be high time for some human

being to enter the abode of the dead to bring about their resurrection" (III, 186). And why should not Father Hyacinth be that man? Why, after the death of his Emily, should not he be the one, the first one, to rise from the dead? "My very life has been snatched away from me forever, without hope, without any consolation in this present existence. Add to this my horrible doubts, my involuntary, irrational doubts which make my heart and my imagination desolate. I have a sort of instinctive perception of the naught of being, the naught of things and of persons. . . . And yet, these doubts are not voluntary, and I should not be able to yield to them without renouncing the Christian faith and even the faith in human nature as I know it from introspection. Such renunciation, however, would amount to moral suicide which in turn would indubitably soon be followed by physical suicide. For, in truth, this game would not be worth the candle: this melancholy game of a life without a *raison d'être*, without a consoling hope" (III, 187). These lines Father Hyacinth wrote to his son Paul, the son whom Emily had born him. To this we might add the observation that doubts are always voluntary, since doubts derive from the will; it is the will which doubts. And our poor Father, in his second childhood, in his second state of virginity, in the eighty-third year of his life, was trying without surcease—another Abisag of Sunam—to bring David back to life.

A few years earlier, at the age of seventy-four, when Father Hyacinth had not yet experienced the death of his wife—the death of his mother— he had believed firmly in "the survival of the souls and their final salvation" (III, 371). He had then stated that "the intellectual power of Renan never transcended doubt" (III, 374). And what about Renan's will? "Renan," he had added, "doubted of everything and—what to my mind is something infinitely sad—he did not die of his doubt but rather continued living on it; he did not suffer from it but rather amused himself with it" (III, 375). I am not so sure about this. At any rate, Father Hyacinth's doubts were the cause of great and prolonged agony. And Renan was well aware of the fact that the truth is sad in its innermost essence.

Father Hyacinth portrayed himself in his fifty-seventh year in this tragic vision, at the site of the Niagara: "My soul is a torrent rushing down from the mountains; its turbulence moves the waters of the years and perhaps of the centuries and, with an ever steeper fall and down ever steeper slopes, it rushes toward death—a catastrophe as formidable as it is inevitable—and further on toward that other abyss which yawns beyond death. It has to follow its course until the creature regains its peace in another kind of dispensation and finds its ultimate stability in the heart of God. Always the problem of *palingenesis* [new birth]. . . . Emily and I will soon experience it. . . ." (II, 251). Neither Rousseau nor Chateaubriand (or rather *René*) nor Sénancour (or rather *Obermann*) have spoken with greater tragic emphasis.

This, then, was Loyson, the man, and Hyacinth, the Father. This was the Christian living the agony of Christianity.

10

CONCLUSION

I am coming to the end of this *opusculum,* because everything in this world—and perhaps even in the other world—must come to an end. But can there be a conclusion, in the usual sense of the term? If the word is understood in the sense of definitive completion, then this end is simultaneously a beginning; and if the word conclusion is understood in the logical sense, then there is no conclusion at all.

I am writing this "conclusion" in physical separation from Spain, my fatherland, a country rent by the most shameless and stupid tyranny, the tyranny of militaristic imbecility; I am writing it away from my home, my family, my eight children—I have as yet no grandchildren—bearing in my heart the pain of civil and religious war. The agony of my dying country has been superimposed in my soul on the agony of Christianity. I feel that politics has been raised to the status of a religion, while simultaneously religion has been debased to the level of politics. I am experiencing the agony of the Spanish Christ, of Christ in His agony. I am experiencing the agony of Europe, of our so-called Christian civilization, of Graeco-Latin and Western Civilization. These two agonies are really one and the same. Christianity and Western Civilization are mutually killing each other. They exist in killing each other.

Meanwhile many believe that a new religion is emerging, a religion which is at once of Jewish and Tartar origin—the religion of Bolshevism: a religion whose prophets are Karl Marx and Dostoevsky. But is Dostoevsky's religion not Christianity? Is *The Brothers Karamazov* not a Gospel?

And meanwhile people say that France, where these lines are being written, the France whose bread I am eating and whose water I am drinking—water which contains the salt of the bones of her dead—that this France is being depopulated and invaded by strangers, because it is a country in which the hunger for maternity and paternity has died because her people no longer believe in the resurrection of the flesh. Do they still believe in the immortality of the soul, in glory, in history? Surely, the agony of the great war must have cured many Frenchmen of their faith in [national] glory.

A few steps only from the place where I am writing, there burns continually, underneath the

Arc de l'Étoile—an arc signifying imperial victory!—the flame lighted upon the tomb of the Unknown Soldier, the soldier whose name will not pass over into history. But is the epithet "unknown" not a name? Is it not worth as much as the name Napoleon Bonaparte? Fathers and mothers who asked themselves whether this unknown soldier might not be their own son, have come to this tomb to pray; Christian mothers and fathers who believe in the resurrection of the flesh. And maybe even unbelieving or atheistic mothers and fathers have come here to pray. And perhaps Christianity will rise again from this tomb.

The poor unknown soldier—who perhaps believed in Christ and in the resurrection of the flesh, or who perhaps was an unbeliever or a rationalist with a faith in the immortality of the soul in history or outside history—sleeps here, dreaming his last dream, covered by stone rather than by the sand of the earth, underneath the huge slabs of a large door which is never opened or closed and upon which are engraved the names of the glories of the Empire. Glories? I wonder.

Not many days ago I was present at a patriotic ceremony: a public procession which filed past this tomb of the unknown soldier. Close by these bones—which are "enstoned" rather than "interred"—stood the President of the Republic of the goddess France, joined by the members of the French government and numerous retired generals in civilian clothes, all of them overshadowed by the stones which in their inscriptions proclaim the bloody glories of the Empire. And this poor unknown soldier was perhaps a boy whose heart and head were filled with history or who maybe detested history.

After the official procession had passed and the first magistrate of the goddess France and his companions had returned to their homes, and after the cries of the nationalists and communists, who had put on a demonstration in the afternoon, had died down, some poor believing mother— one of those who believe in the virginal maternity of Mary—approached silently and alone the tomb of the unknown soldier and prayed: "Thy kingdom come!" She prayed for the arrival of that kingdom which is not of this world. And she went on: "Hail Mary, full of grace, the Lord is with thee; blessed art thou amongst women and blessed be the fruit of thy womb, Jesus. Holy Mary, Mother of God; pray for us sinners, now and in the hour of our death. Amen!" Such a prayer was never offered on the steps of the Acropolis [of Athens]! And all of Christian France joined in the prayer of this mother. And the poor unknown son—for all we know—listened to this prayer as he went to his death and dreamed that his home would live on in heaven, in the heaven of his fatherland, his sweet France, and that the aeons of her eternity would be rekindled by the kisses of his mother and by the kiss of the light emanating from the Mother of God.

Facing the tomb of the unknown Frenchman—who is something more sacred than the average Frenchman—I experienced the agony of Christianity in France.

There are moments when one imagines that Europe and the entire civilized world are standing on the threshold of a new millennium; that the end of the civilized world, the end of civilization, is near, just as the early Christians, the true evangelical Christians, believed that the end of the world was at hand. And some may feel inclined to repeat the tragic Portuguese saying, *"Isto da vontade de morrer"* (this cauess a yearning for death).

And so we witness the establishment of the Society of Nations, the United States of Civilization in Geneva, under the shadows of Calvin and Jean-Jacques [Rousseau]. And also under the shadow of Amiel, who is smiling sadly in contemplating—from what distance?—this political edifice. And still another shadow is smiling sadly, the shadow of Wilson, who also was a Christian politician, another contradiction-made-flesh, another contradiction-made-spirit. Wilson, the mystic of peace, was as great a contradiction incarnate as the first Moltke, the mystic of war.

The hurricane of madness which is sweeping over a large part of European civilization appears

150   THE AGONY OF CHRISTIANITY

to be a kind of insanity which physicians are able to specify as to its origin and nature. Many of the agitators and dictators, the men who carry the masses with them, are in the early stages of progressive paralysis. They represent the suicide of the flesh. There are even some people who believe that we are dealing here with the mystery of iniquity.

But let us look once more at that firmly ingrained tradition which identifies the biblical sin of our first parents—their tasting of the fruit from the tree of the knowledge of good and evil—with the sin of the flesh which yearns to rise again. But the fact is that the flesh is no longer preoccupied with resurrection, no longer motivated by any hunger and thirst for paternity and maternity, but by mere pleasure and lust. The font of life is poisoned, and this poison has infected the font of knowledge.

In Hesiod's "The Labors and the Days," which is a poem of greater significance than the Homeric texts, we are told that under the reign of peace, when the earth will be prolific in the production of life, the leaves of the oak tree will bear acorns, its trunk will nurse the bees, the woolly sheep will bear lambs, and "women will give birth to sons who will resemble their fathers (ἐοικότα τέχνα γονεῦσιν, verses 232-235). This does not seem to mean *legitimate* sons but rather well built sons (cf. Hesiod, *Les travaux et les jours. Édition nouvelle par Paul Mazon*. Paris: Hachette, 1914;

note to verse 235, p. 81). Well built sons or, more precisely, healthy sons.

On a certain occasion I had a talk with an old peasant, a poor mountain-dweller, in the vicinity of the Hurdes, that region in the center of Spain which is supposed to be quite uncivilized. I asked him whether it was true that the people there were living in promiscuity. He wanted to know what that meant, and when I explained it to him he replied: "No, no longer; but it was different in my youth. When all mouths are clean, people can afford drinking out of the same cup. At that time jealousy was something unknown. Jealousy came together with those illnesses which poison the blood and turn people into fools and idiots. You see, one cannot allow people to make children who will be fools and idiots and will not be good for anything." This peasant spoke like a sage. And perhaps he spoke like a Christian. At any rate, he did not speak like one of those married men in the dramas of Calderon de la Barca, married men who are tormented by that sense of honor which is not a Christian but a pagan sentiment.

In the words of that old and laconic man of the mountains I could sense the tragedy of original sin and simultaneously the tragedy of Christianity and of all that the dogma of the Immaculate Conception of the Blessed Virgin Mary implies. The Mother of God, who revives the dead, must be exempt from original sin.

And in the words of that old and laconic man of the mountains I sensed also the tragedy of our civilization. And I remembered Nietzsche.

But is the sin of the flesh really the most execrable sin? Is it truly the original sin?

For St. Paul the most execrable sin is avarice. And the reason is that avarice mistakes the means for the end. But what is meant by "means"? And what is the meaning of "end"? What and where is the finality of life? There is such a thing as avarice of the spirit and avarice of maternity and paternity.

Kant postulated as the supreme principle of morality that we regard our neighbors as ends in themselves, never as means. This was his way of translating the saying, "Love your neighbor as you love your own self." But Kant was a bachelor, a monk in the world, a miser. Was he a Christian? Maybe he mistook himself for an absolute end. Human generation came to an end in him. "Love your neighbor as you love your own self?" And how must we love our own selves?

But joined to this terrible physical sickness is a sickness of the soul, the offspring of spiritual avarice—envy! Envy is the sickness of Cain, the sickness of Judas Iscariot and, if we believe Dante, the sickness of Brutus and Cassius. Cain did not kill Abel because of his brother's economic prosperity but because he was envious of the grace which Abel had found before God; nor did Judas sell his master for the thirty pieces of silver but because he was an avaricious and envious miser.

I am writing these lines in physical separation from my beloved Spain; but Spain, my daughter, the Spain of the resurrection and of immortality, is at my side, even here in France, in the lap of this my France, which nourishes my flesh and my spirit, my resurrection and my immortality. And together with the agony of Christianity I feel within myself the agony of my Spain and the agony of my France. And I say to Spain and to France and through them to all Christendom and to all the rest of humanity: "May the kingdom of God come to us! . . . Holy Mary, Mother of God, pray for us sinners, now and in the hour of our death." Now, now, in the hour of our agony!

"Christianity is like the cholera which ravages a land to carry away a certain number of chosen people, and thereafter it disappears," Father Hyacinth heard M. Gazier, the last of the Jansenists, pronounce these words on the occasion of a banquet—a symposium—given on January 25, 1880. Is civilization not another disease which carries off its elect by virtue of their folly? Cholera, after all, fells men swiftly. For M. Gazier, Christianity was a disease. And perhaps these two sicknesses are at bottom one and the same disease. And the nature of the disease [in both, Christianity and civilization] is the inherent contradiction.

As I have said, I am writing these lines in

physical separation from my beloved Spain, in separation from my mother and my daughter— yes, my daughter, for I am one of her fathers—; I am writing these lines while my country lies in agony and while simultaneously Christianity itself lies in agony in my country. Spain wanted to propagate Catholicism by means of the sword; she proclaimed a crusade, and she is going to die by the sword, and by a poisoned sword at that! The agony of my Spain is the agony of my Christianity. And the agony of my own Quixotism is the agony of Don Quixote.

A few days ago, some poor deluded people whom the Council of War had acquitted, were strangled to death. They were strangled because the reign of terror demanded it. They are fortunate indeed that they were not killed by being shot! For when I once told the King of Spain that we must do away with the death penalty in order to do away with the hangman, he replied: "But this kind of punishment exists in almost every country! Just take a look at the French Republic. We are fortunate here that we inflict capital punishment without the shedding of blood. . . ." He was of course referring to our method of strangulation [by means of an iron collar] as compared with the guillotine. But Christ hung in agony and died on the cross shedding His blood, and my beloved Spain lies in agony and may be dying on the cross of the sword and shedding her blood. . . . Will it be redeeming blood? Perhaps the blood will wash away the poison.

But Christ did shed His blood not only on the cross—that blood which baptized Longinus, the blind soldier, and made him believe, but "His sweat fell to the ground like thick drops of blood" ὡσεὶ θρόμβοι αἵματος during His agony on the Mount of Olives (Luke 22:44). And these drops, resembling drops of blood, were the seeds of agony, the seeds of the agony of Christianity. And meanwhile Christ sighed, "Not my will, but Thy will be done!" (Luke 22:42) Oh Christ, our Christ, why hast Thou forsaken us?

Paris, December 1924.